GROUP MEDITATION

ALSO BY MICHAEL LIPSON

Stairway of Surprise: Six Steps to a Creative Life

GROUP MEDITATION

Michael Lipson, Ph.D.

SteinerBooks
2011

Published by SteinerBooks/Anthroposophic Press
610 Main Street, Great Barrington, MA 01230
www.steinerbooks.org

Cover image: Ross Bleckner, *Galaxy With Birds,*
1993; oil on linen, 60 x 84 in.; collection of
the Fisher Landau Center for Art
Book design by William Jens Jensen

FSC
Mixed Sources
Product group from well-managed
forests and other controlled sources

Cert no. SW-COC-002283
www.fsc.org
© 1996 Forest Stewardship Council

LIBRARY OF CONGRESS CATALOGING-IN-PUBLICATION DATA

Lipson, Michael, 1957–
 Group meditation / Michael Lipson.
  p. cm.
 Includes bibliographical references.
 ISBN 978-0-88010-730-3
 1. Meditation. I. Title.
 BL627.L58 2011
 204'.35—dc22

                                   2010050534

Printed in the United States of America

CONTENTS

Peace I leave with you, my peace I give to you.
Not as the world gives, give I to you.
John 14:27

PREFACE

This book comes from joy. To meditate in a group is one of the greatest pleasures I know. When we find ourselves, in silent meditation, interweaving with each other and with the very fabric of the universe, it is not a neutral experience. It may involve a quiet and welcome relief from suffering, a sense of touching the Ground, but it can also bring shattering experiences that bless us with opening and presence.

As we immerse ourselves in the meditative theme, we touch on the trinity as the ancient Indians knew it: *Sat-Chit-Ananda,* or "Being-Consciousness-Bliss." *Being:* we taste existence itself at a heightened pitch of intensity. It comes as a fresh shock that there is something, this world with these people for instance—when there could so easily be nothing. *Consciousness:* we are aware of ourselves and of the world as significances, expressions, with awareness permeating the all of it. It becomes a universe of living, meaningful beings rather than dead, meaningless things. *Bliss:* we revel in this freshly existent world of awarenesses, increasing our gratitude at creation—in spite of everything.

The book you hold in your hands has the aim of stimulating this being, consciousness, and bliss through group meditation. The first half of the book deals with the concept of group meditation in the logos or meaning-oriented style, and therefore with the peace that passes understanding. The second half of the book offers specific guidance in the practice of group meditation. While it is shorter than the first half in numbers of pages, repeated practice of its suggestions will make it seem long enough.

Individual meditation is good, and can even offer a complete path in itself. Group meditation enormously heightens our capacity to be, ourselves, the news from Heaven.

PART ONE
THEORY OF GROUP MEDITATION

What is Meditation?

Our consciousness is capable of transforming itself. This is possible because consciousness is not a closed system, but open to wider spheres and capable of improvisation. Meditation is one way to awaken this transformative capacity and to grow, as David Spangler says, "more in love with the world."

There are many practices known as meditation. Today, they are often sold to consumers under the guise of physical and emotional medicine. Meditation is supposed to lower blood pressure, refresh you from a stressful life, and offer a thousand other personal benefits.

Those who originated the traditions of meditation and prayer would never have stooped so low. Whether in Buddhism, Christianity, Judaism, Taoism, Hinduism, or Islam, the originators of prayer and meditation had much more ecological goals in mind. They would have said that meditation unites the human with the source of creation, and awakens us to our own true nature and that of the universe. They were, in many cases, prepared to die for their beliefs and practices. It would never have occurred to them to make the goal of meditation either the physical health or emotional wellbeing of individuals who undertake it.

The original purpose of meditation and prayer was literally *re-ligious:* to link back together the heavens and the Earth. There are therefore two goals to meditation. On the one hand, it gives the meditant a different sense of self, a sense of knowing at last one's true nature. On the other hand, it opens us to new, higher intuitions about the world. Perhaps there is only one goal of meditation.

To achieve its natural aim, meditation asks us to exercise and strengthen our attention, in principle, limitlessly. Attention, concentration, focus, immersion: these are the cognitive face of love. Their exercise involves disregarding distractions of all kinds and diving headlong into whichever theme we choose to meditate. In other words, meditation depends for its power on the quality of the consciousness in question, not on the apparent content of the meditation.

Still, we arrive at new registers of consciousness just by forgetting our own consciousness and its quality and instead letting the chosen theme of meditation be all in all. In meditating, nothing exists for us but the theme. Moreover, with such exclusive focus, the theme grows. We diminish as separate selves, only to find ourselves renewed in the new context of the theme as it emerges. As Emerson put it, writing about his experience of nature, "I am nothing; I see all. I become a transparent eyeball." It is precisely through the dissolution of our separate selves that we can awaken as integrated selves, re-linked to the whole. Moreover, what this whole is, what the universe is, changes in surprising ways through our act of concentrating on the theme.

Meditation challenges us. It dares us to let go of who we think we are and what we think the world is, even what we think thinking is. In the process of working our way into the theme, we feel this challenge; we feel the cost. It can be thrilling, but it requires tremendous renunciation too—"costing not less than everything," as T. S. Eliot wrote. Along the way, we find that meditation does not flatter, but instead presents the meditant with glaring evidence of his or her flaws. As one Tibetan master put it, "Meditation is one insult after another." As long as we can be insulted, an active meditative practice will confront us with our selfishness.

The kind of meditation described in this book always has do with a theme, each time chosen by the meditant, a theme that, in the course of our work, we come to understand differently. The logos, or Word, mentioned earlier has to do with understanding, on the receptive side, which is the same as meaning, on the expressive side. In meditative practice, we reach beyond customary understandings and meanings. We come to understand the meditative theme at its origin, or closer to its origin. If we then communicate our experience in terms adequate to our understanding, we mean what we say at a more intimate and powerful register of speech. The words may not be different, but we mean more by them. Whether listening or speaking, receiving or expressing, we know that words are only indications, hints, at the subtle and tremendous reach of the theme.

When Mephistopheles disguises himself as Faust in Goethe's play and gives devilish advice to a young university student, he tells him, "Stick to the words themselves." In meditation, we go in just the opposite direction from this disastrous suggestion. We start with the words or the images of the theme, but we do not stop there. We pursue them upstream, toward their source. We want to find the place, and have the experience, from out of which the author of the meditative theme was writing—whether Mohammed, Moses, or St. John. If the theme is something taken from nature—a stone, a landscape—then we are seeking the generative idea, even the generative being, that invented and sustains the stone or landscape.

Heraclitus, the logos-oriented initiator of Western philosophy, said that the soul has a logos that grows of itself. He was marveling at the very quality we meet in every good-enough meditation—that it takes on a life of its own. This is very different from the ping-ponging of associations and distractions normally considered to be thinking. Meditation brings news, not always by giving us a different content, but by self-renewing and deepening content we thought we knew.

Meditation therefore gives us nothing we can keep. We may want something to keep, but really, that is a hopeless and unworthy goal. There is no bottom line or take-home message or list of deliverables or even useful tool that we should get from meditation. There is nothing to get. There is nothing in it for us. Meditation gives "not as the world gives," but through gifts that instantly dissolve and must be rediscovered afresh each time we meditate.

Nor is there any fixed "how" to meditation. We have techniques, of course, and methods, and notions about how to do it. This book outlines some of these. Yet techniques are always inadequate, out of date the moment they are formulated. The only valid method is your current, newly invented finding of the theme. The theologian Friedrich Gogarten put it this way:

> One can have this knowledge only while one is permitting it to
> be given to him and while one is receiving it from the One who
> discloses it to him.

In this, he echoes Rudolf Steiner, who, in his primary philosophical work, *The Philosophy of Freedom,* made the same comment about the peculiar freshness required for spiritual knowledge:

> Once achieved, this view can become part of the very life of the soul itself. But no theoretical answer is given that, once acquired, is simply carried as a conviction preserved by memory. Such an answer would have to be an illusion, according to the style of thought underlying this book. Therefore, no such finished, closed-off answer is provided here; rather, reference is made to a region of soul experience in which, through the soul's inner activity, the question answers itself in a living way, always anew, whenever a human being needs it.

In normal understanding, we more or less have the sense that we are doing it, making it. We rarely focus on the part of the process that is receptive. Actually, understanding of all kinds depends on a combination of activity and receptivity, though we are typically aware of only the active pole. It is precisely when cognitive activity becomes most active, however, that it is also most receptive. At the peak of willing and intending and working toward the theme of our understanding, the gesture of will reverses and we find that we are being thought, being understood, being formed and informed, from "outside." We say, in effect, "Thy will be done." It is for this reason that no finished form of understanding feels adequate. A finished form would be something we have rather than something currently being given—and only such current giving is the experience in question.

Much of the nature of the meditative gesture is condensed in a story about the Buddha's awakening. He had long engaged in ascetic practices, torturing the body, but realized that a middle way existed between physical indulgence and asceticism. This way involved a three-fold realization: that reality is alive and ever changing; that clinging leads to suffering; that there is no self separate from the world. When a local woman brought him a bowl of rice, he broke his fast by eating it. Coomaraswamy tells the story:

> She finds the Bodhisattva seated beneath the tree, and gives him the rice in a golden bowl, and a golden ewer of water. She receives his blessings. He then goes down to the river to bathe, after which he eats the food, which is to last him for seven weeks. He casts the bowl into the river, and from the significant fact that it floats upstream he learns that he will succeed that very day.

We empty our bowl so that it can become receptive. This takes effort. At some point, though, all striving ends, and we cast our receptivity into the stream of the cosmic river of existence. Against all probability, against all previous experience, against the grain of all cognitive habits, our receptive attention moves backward up the flow of meaning, toward the very origin. Meditation carries us upstream.

What Is a Group?

There can be no socioeconomic, racial, or "faith"-based criterion for participation in a meditation group. There is nothing you have to know, or believe in, to be a full, active participant. What makes it a group is none of these external elements. Nor does long acquaintance among the group members make it a group in a meditative sense.

A group may have a kind of leader, yet only in the sense of someone who mostly chooses the themes, or has more experience in meditation. The true leader of the group is the truth of the moment, which can speak now from this one, now from that one. In any case, the structure of meditation described in the second section makes clear that there is no room, in this style of meditation, for anything in the way of group suggestion or coercion. The members of the group support one another in many ways by their common striving, and there can be astonishing similarities between what people come to in their meditations, and yet each person's work and each person's insights arrive in a completely individual, freely achieved manner. No one is forcing anyone, or "leading" anyone in a negative sense.

Our unity-in-diversity comes rather in those moments when we know, by direct experience, of our shared root in the heavens. Here on Earth, that is, in normal consciousness, we may seem separate. In heaven, which is to say in the superconscious sources of awareness, we are together. This does not mean leaving the Earth, at all, but rather finding its true nature. As Thérèse of Lisieux suggested on her deathbed, "I am not going anywhere. I am arriving."

> It is given to very few spirits to realize that things and beings really exist. From earliest childhood, I have desired nothing other than the full revelation of this fact before I die. It seems to me that you too are engaged in this quest. (Simone Weil, letter to Joë Bousquet)

Who we are to one another remains mysterious until we release everything in us that obscures it. Releasing distraction after distraction, plunging with our best powers into the theme of the meditation, we can grow in clarity and find that what was previously mysterious or obscure has become, or always was, utterly evident. Romano Guardini spoke of the "mystery in what is utterly clear." It was an open secret all along, hidden in plain view.

By focusing together on a high theme, we relax the boundaries between us without even thinking of this as a project, and find we are already united in the ever-more-evident truth. This is why the Quakers were originally called not simply the Society of Friends, but the Religious Society of Friends of the Truth. It was their primary friendship with the truth that made them able to befriend one another. "Truth" in this sense does not refer to a fixed body of knowledge or belief, of course, but to a process of opening and receiving.

In Greek legend, there is a river, Lethe, which we must cross as we move from the heavenly realms to the Earth. At birth, as we dip into this water, we forget all that we knew from before, from the time when we still participated in the weave of the world. That is why the Greek word for truth does not refer to some correspondence between what is in our minds and a fixed outer world, but instead to lifting the amnesia into which our birth has placed us. The ancient word they invented for truth was *a-letheia*—the undoing of Lethe's spell. Truth is an *unforgetting*. Socrates, in the Meno dialogue, states that we need only remember ourselves, and all that is will be open to us.

The passage through Lethe by which we forget our participation in the universe is also the spell of forgetting by which we imagine ourselves separate from one another and locked in distinct physical bodies. In the active remembering known as meditation, we find that truth itself makes us friends.

THE LIGHT

Many traditions tell us that the world began as light and will end as light.

Sometimes this primal, final light is represented not visually but aurally, as silence. Sometimes it is represented as a syllable or sound, or by other names and images. Sometimes it is called "nothing," or "emptiness"; but then it would have to be a very special nothing, an emptiness filled with possibility.

As light, too, it is no ordinary brightness, no object that aids in dualistic understanding, but rather the very essence of understanding. The light is not something that exists. Light is being itself. Light does not mean something other than itself; it is the very possibility of meaning. Again, the light does not make us happy. Light *is* happiness.

What is this light? Imagine you are with friends discussing a difficult topic by firelight while camping in the woods. It is a cloudy, moonless night. Someone douses the fire and now you are all in pitch darkness. Yet the discussion goes on. At some point, you might very well say, "OK, thanks. That sheds some light on the topic." What kind of light are you talking about? All physical light is gone, and the topic itself may be dark, like betrayal or grief. Yet the light of understanding is there—not as a metaphor. Understanding is the original light, for which the light of the Sun, for instance, is itself only a metaphor.

External light, from the Sun or a lamp, is at best only the emblem of the primal light, which is what makes clear, lets be, and is transparent to itself. In some languages, the Earth, or the universe as a whole, is called by a word that means "light" (in Russian, *mir,* and Rumanian, *lumia*). It would never occur to us today to call the world by that name. For us, the world is dark. We seem at times to be an all-but-impenetrable darkness to ourselves. Even more dark are our relations with one another.

This does not mean in any way that this world is bad or evil, or that it is our goal to flee it, or that life is better elsewhere or elsewhen. When we see the world as darkness we are misunderstanding it—a misunderstanding with a long history and deeply embedded within us, like a thorn in the flesh.

Here is Kafka, not normally thought of as a mystic but, still, a spiritual reader of the world, in his amazing collection *On Sin, Suffering, Hope, and the True Way:*

> There exists nothing other than a spiritual world. What we call the sensory world is the evil in the spiritual world, and what we call evil is only a necessary moment in our eternal development.

And here is Steiner, in a closely related and provocative comment from chapter 25 of the *Autobiography:* "The sensory world is not really illusory, but the human being makes it so."

The long-term promise of the great spiritual traditions is that once again the universe could become light in light. Then there would be nothing un-meaning, nothing un-creative, nothing fixed and dead to interrupt the circulation of the living light. In this possibility, there could be only meanings and makers of meaning, with no external world "in" which they need to find a place.

There would be no fixity at all—no fixity of meaning, for example—but rather a universe of continuous improvisation. Human beings would not act at random and in perpetual discord, but in creative dissonance and harmony. We would know one another and all conscious entities as beings of light—creators and receivers of fresh meaning, changing or self-renewing at every instant. All along the way of this Earth-enlivened path, the world and the people we meet matter more to us; they become more interesting; they stimulate more questions along with more certainties.

The First Letter of John the Evangelist, in which God is called "light," is the very letter in which he also declares, "God is love." If these are not just pretty words, what do they mean? What does it mean to say that the origin of the apparently solid world is "light" and, at the same time, "love" and (from the same author) "Word"?

The aim of group meditation, as of every spiritual striving, can be characterized accordingly. We aim to realize ourselves and the world as continuing the originary love/light/Word. We do not merely discover or know about, but we ourselves become the living, still-productive source. We have already spoken about openness in this regard. It is important to note, though, that there would be no one to experience all this if there were not also boundaries of some kind that make us *us*—that is, independent beings even while we relax our boundaries to become more open. We do not have the goal of dissolving utterly and in every way. Rather, we come to discover that our true, unitive nature is very unlike our separative self-imagining. Wallace Stevens spoke of "ghostlier demarcations"—boundaries that allow more conversation to get through.

The various traditions hint at the light, or ground of being, in various ways, but they are unmistakably referring to the same thing, and often have the same kind of challenge about them. The nineteenth-century Zen Master Kokushi referred to the light without using that term:

> A way to approach the fundamental knowledge is to set aside all
> such interpretations and focus intensive non-conceptual inquiry
> on the state where this setting-aside has taken place.

It is on this precondition of release, or the true, universe-shattering humility, that we can sometimes have an experience of the theme of meditation that is really neither "inside" nor "outside," but both and neither. As noted, we can experience the world and ourselves before they are split apart but, more particularly, before the split, widespread in Western culture since at least René Descartes, between mental and physical reality. In our day, it is popular to resolve this split by saying that mind stuff, like thoughts and emotions, are "really" only brain events, therefore physical and spatial. In some times and cultures, of course, it has seemed obvious on the contrary that the physical world is itself a mental or spiritual thing if it has reality at all. However, the logos/light experienced in meditation is neither of these, but the primordial condition for the possibility of either. It is more solid than thought, but more meaningful than matter. When you experience it, you will be surprised both by how unlike every normal category it seems and, paradoxically, by how at home you feel in it. Zen masters called it "the natural state."

All this may sound like a far-distant or impossibly lofty goal, but in some respects it requires only that we return to the miraculous features of everyone's early childhood. As Goethe said, "Every child is a genius." One way to characterize this genius would be to say that, originally, children live exclusively in the logos-world, the world of meanings.

I once worked with the mother of two girls from a large African-American family. She told me that when they were little, the girls loved their Uncle George. They knew him as a lively, engaging family member, fun to play with at the yearly reunions. Now Uncle George happened to be Caucasian. It was at a family picnic on the beach, when the girls were 6 and 8 or so, that one of them looked up at George flipping burgers at the grill and said in astonishment, "Uncle George! You're white!" "Yes," he answered, "That's a fact." The point is that, up until then, they had not noticed. For them Uncle George was sufficiently known as his meanings: his love, his joking, the gesture with which he flipped a burger. He was perceived more deeply still, perhaps, in his fundamental unity. He was certainly not just a body among bodies, a thing among things, until that moment of recognition and descent when he became white.

When, for us, both the apparently physical world and all souls become like Uncle George before he was white, then we will be well on our way back to the world of logos. This will be return with a difference. Originally, we were all together in the light, but we were asleep. Now we are separate, and fallen into darkness, but painfully awake. Ultimately, we will be awake and together in the light. And only then beginning.

Whole Giving

Meditation worthy of the name is not an adornment, then, a talent to acquire or knowledge to have, or an aid to wellbeing. Rather, meditation takes us to a limit where we ask the questions asked of us by life, not conceptually, but with our whole selves.

This means setting aside, or sacrificing, or (it may feel like) killing, much more of ourselves than we are initially ready to release. Often, the Spirit, God, the ground of being, is described only negatively, since the old writers knew very well we are constantly looking to acquire, while the light becomes visible just to the extent that we divest.

A hint in this direction comes, too, from such sources as the 1984 Iron Man competition in Hawaii, in which a very young physical-education major, Julie Moss, competed without adequate training. Having been in the lead for most of the three events (swimming, cycling, running a marathon), she was only yards from the finish line when she suddenly could go no farther and fell in a dead faint. She had not trained, paced herself, or even eaten adequately that day. She tried then to get up, and struggled a few more steps, but fell helplessly, unable even to break the fall with her arms. She fell as if dead, and many observers thought her dead. She could not go on. She had defecated in her pants. She had lost all dignity and hope. She was finished.

From nowhere, she says when she tells the story, a voice addressed her. "Get up!" it said—a merciless, or at least an inhumanly stern voice. She protested that she could not, but the voice kept repeating, "Get up." Until, out of nowhere, she found she could crawl forward. An inch at a time she crawled the last yards to the finish. What made her rise to her knees? How could she do that? Why even bother, when she was now clearly losing and others were finishing ahead of her?

Instead of answering these questions, I want to focus on the video, still visible on YouTube, of Julie Moss crossing the finish line on that now-famous day, though the video is strangely dark. There are too many people crowding around in the dim light; there is noise and confusion; most people do not notice her; the film just doesn't present it as a glorious moment. For Julie, however, and for the onlookers who understood what was going on, it was one of the most beautiful and impressive moments they had ever witnessed, a moment that still reduces them to tears when they describe it. Outwardly, all was lost. Outwardly, it stayed lost, or at least lame. However, the inner victory, after total abandonment and impotence, made her "loss" of the competition infinitely more successful than all her subsequent professional successes. She had reached what T. S. Eliot in "Little Gidding" calls "A condition of complete simplicity/(Costing not less than everything)."

In ancient times, and still today, most forms of prayer and meditation involve putting to rest the normal use of the body and mind. This was symbolized by placing the palms together, for example, or sitting in the lotus position, or lying prostrate. All these are not tokens of humility or obeisance in first order, but indications that the hands will not be used for the plough, or the legs for walking, for the time being. Instead, the energies that used to go into such activities will now be devoted entirely to the prayer or meditation at hand. This involves an addition beyond the attention required for everyday, practical thinking. It means that the very life and movement normally proper to the body will now be invested in the meditation. The forces needed even for breathing and the circulation of the blood are, in some traditions, briefly devoted to the object of prayer. We can recall Wordsworth: "Until the breath of this corporeal frame, / And even the motion of our human blood / Almost suspended, we are laid asleep / In body and become a living soul." Something similar can happen even in profane moments: "We waited with bated breath." "His blood froze." At death, all the energies that were used to maintain a physical body are, in principal, available to meet divinity.

In attempting repeatedly to give ourselves more and more completely to the theme of meditation, we find that this means simply giving our whole attention. To give one's whole attention is to give one's whole self.

PEACE

If by some strange chance peace prevailed all over the world for a few days, with no armed or unarmed conflict of any kind, we know that it could not last—not if human beings were still as they are today. To the extent that we see ourselves as separate from one another, as belonging to groups with opposed interests, as having fixed beliefs, we will necessarily return to conflict in short order. Lasting peace requires that we develop a different disposition; that our inner structure be revised.

To put it in a formula, we could say that the precondition for horizontal peace—that is, peace among humans and human groups—is vertical peace. This vertical peace means the dissolution of the wall that divides us from the heavens above our minds and the Earth below our feet. It involves a revisioning of what a human being is, a changed mind, changed senses, and an ever-new openness to the influx of intuition.

When the heavens and Earth are open to us, when we can effectively look upward and downward, then we will also be able to look sideways without grasping or aversion.

Our current human configuration involves both openness and closedness. The openness consists in our being able to receive new ideas from time to time, to enjoy a new kind of humor, to love someone new, to forgive, to be surprised. Our closedness consists in our attachment to habit in all its forms.

Though we have both open and closed features, in terms of a sense of self we tend to identify most of all with something fixed or closed about ourselves. We identify, for example, with being male or female, old or young, American or Kenyan, and so on. These identifications are important, worthwhile, and cannot be ignored. In fact, if we did not develop such identifications, we would never be fully human.

The possibility exists, however, while fully respecting our incarnate particularity, to identify gradually more with our openness, with the unfinished, with the possible. This shift in identification toward the open happens whenever we relax our boundaries and take an intentional risk in any area of human consciousness. All of the functions of consciousness—sensory perception, memory, mental imagery, dreaming, thinking, feeling, and action—can be opened up so that they no longer conceal their own sources. They can all be the site of an intentional risk, in which we make ourselves available to the new.

When this process goes far enough, we find that "sideways" and "upward" are themselves no longer separate. Vertical and horizontal peace are one. The heavens are present in our seeing, hearing, thinking, feeling and so on. There is nowhere to leave Earth for, and no need to leave Earth. We find ourselves strengthened in our individuality and particularity by the very fact of feeling ourselves embedded in the matrix of all that is. The "Earth" and our "self" are not closed systems, but open windows through which blow an infinity of forces and beings.

When the risen Christ says, "My peace I give you," he means this very peace between horizontal and vertical consciousness, imaged by a cross. The one who has gone through the most radical separateness has the capacity for the greatest unity. In this peace, there is no longer a division between heavens and Earth, between human and divine consciousness. Rather, there is an endless possibility of communication among realms that currently seem closed off from one another.

When two nations are at peace, they have embassies in one another's territory. They have conversations. In times of war, the embassies close. You bring all your people home, and you send their people packing. If peace returns, the embassies may open again, allowing for communication, commerce, even intermarriage. This is how it is with us and the heavens. To have peace in this sense, imagine an embassy within you into which you invite the heavenly hosts. Imagine an embassy in the heavens where you send advance diplomats to establish friendly relations. Be willing for a nonverbal conversation to arise.

CONCENTRATION

It is given to us to turn ourselves toward a theme or object of our choice. No human individuals create the miraculous capacity to concentrate. We simply find we can do it. We can direct our attention at will, at least to some degree. Nor do we know how we do it. As soon as we have the idea of it, we have the power for it in our hands.

Take a thought such as the thought of triangles. What do you know about triangles? Give yourself a full sixty-second minute to think about them with your eyes closed. Go ahead.

Well? Did you come up with some thoughts about triangles? Perhaps that they have three sides as well as three angles. Perhaps that the sum of the internal angles is 180 degrees, the equivalent of a straight line. Perhaps that there are three kinds of triangles: scalene, isosceles, and equilateral. Perhaps something about right-angled triangles and the Pythagorean theorem.

Perhaps in that minute you had distractions, too, including extraneous thoughts such as, "When will the minute end?" Or "When is lunchtime?" Or, "What is the point of this exercise?" Or, "I don't care about triangles."

The miracle of concentration consists first in this: that in spite of distractions, somehow you could think a few thoughts about a triangle. You just set the process in motion with a modicum of good will, and true thoughts come. You are the beneficiary of a process you did not invent and cannot eradicate: the capacity to open your attention toward a theme and so to have the theme grow.

Here is another aspect of the miracle. True concentration is at the same time improvisation. It does not give you the same thought again and again. That would be memory, and it would soon become boring. If you are really concentrated on a theme, it either gives you entirely new contents from moment to moment or else it gives you old contents afresh, so that you do not even notice that they have been thought before. Whenever we do notice that they are old thoughts, we are not concentrating.

And here is another aspect. The more concentrated you are, the less you notice yourself and the fact that you are concentrated. When I am busy trying hard to concentrate, I am far from concentrated. As attention grows stronger, I seem to disappear as a separate self, forget to notice myself, forget (along with everything else) even to evaluate whether the attention is strong or weak. As John the Baptist said, "I must decrease and he must increase." That is, the concentrating or attending self disappears from view, while whatever is being attended to, increases. There's less you, more world. And the world (in this case, the meditation theme) grows in several ways: in presence, significance, variety, quality, and in the intensity of its being. What diminishes is its abstraction, its separateness.

A high degree of concentration is possible for us, at least for moments, and again we can find models for it in the abilities of young children. When kindergartners listen to a fairy tale or watch a puppet show, I have seen them literally drool in their self-forgetful immersion as the story unfolds before their mind's eye. They no longer notice their bodies at all, or the room, or the other people. Instead, they get the benefit of all these elements just by forgetting them and sharing the life of the story itself, as it plays out in its own world.

Notice that when your mind is not focused but distracted, this state involves a lot of "concentration" in a certain sense. You may suddenly find you have gotten home from work, but you didn't notice the drive or the walk at all. Your mind was absorbed in a daydream, a worry, a plan, a conversation you were rehashing. Rather than thinking of this only as a fault, an absence of attention to your current project of driving home, for instance, we can switch figure and ground and see that the mind was indeed absorbed, only not intentionally. You managed to be so involved in what you were "thinking" about that the sensory world fell away: you didn't notice the road, the other cars, the birdsong, the moment of turning off the ignition.

Though you forgot the world around you, however, you probably did not quite forget your self in the daydream. Daydreams and distractions tend only to emphasize the everyday self, indulging its self-involvement even through fantasies and memories of pain. By meditative practice, we can achieve the total level of absorption of a daydream, but now intentionally. It is a kind of absorption that lets both the perceptual world we thought we knew, and our own habitual self-preoccupation, fall away.

MEDITATION ON A THEME

The desire for meditation to put us in a different state accords with our current style of living. We want to be at peace, in love, ecstatic, or simply quiet and healthy. In this way, we want meditation to do for us what we want drugs and alcohol to do for us. We want it to take us away from our troubles and put us someplace better.

The original and most satisfying style of meditation, however, does not aim at a particular state of mind or soul or heart—even though it does, in practice, alter all of these, precisely without aiming to do so. Instead of orienting toward a state, meditation orients us toward meaning. It has us focus initially on a specific content, which is the meaning—really a whole web of relationship and implication—of the chosen theme in any given episode of meditation. The content eventually grows very unlike the contents of our everyday consciousness, of course, and in fact the content, no matter how vast and how special, is also not the ultimate aim of meditation.

Ancient shamanic prayers, the Vedas and the Upanishads, the Buddhist sutras, the Zen koans, the blessings and prayers of Jewish and Christian liturgy, were all originally aimed at specific non-normal understandings. They asked the human reciting them to speak and think out of a more unified awareness: both unified within itself and in unity with the world. It is an awareness "far more deeply interfused," as Wordsworth put it:

> A presence that disturbs me with the joy
> Of elevated thoughts, a sense sublime
> Of something far more deeply interfused
> Whose dwelling is the light of setting suns,
> And the round ocean and the living air,
> And the blue sky, and in the mind of man;
> A motion and a spirit, that impels
> All thinking things, all objects of all thought,
> And rolls through all things.

When we meditate now, it is appropriate to choose a theme that we suspect has a high or profound origin. If it is verbal, it must be in a language we understand, so that the lowest rung of its ladder of meanings is accessible to our everyday consciousness. We might take a theme from world scripture or just a sentence or phrase that we guess in advance has a hidden power from above, or a hidden depth from below, that we will attempt to explore. Secular themes of this kind can be found in the work of Ralph Waldo Emerson, for example, or in Rainer Maria Rilke's poetry—anywhere you sense the author was speaking from an immersion that interests you. You are the judge as to whether a sentence is "meditatable" or even worth the time to find out.

The natural world itself is the sign of such higher meanings, and elements of nature can also be taken as meditation themes both by individuals and in groups. Though we will be speaking of meditation mostly in terms of concentration on a verbally given theme, much of what applies to the verbal applies to the "physical," because the world is word-like through and through.

Another kind of meditative theme is not a sentence or a symbol or the natural world, but rather an emblematic event. Such events are the healings in the Gospels or the Buddhist Jataka tales or the story of the Bhagavad Gita. If we choose an event as our theme, it is not a verbal formula or an imagination of the event that is our proper aim, but the meaning and sequence of the event as a whole.

KINDS OF THEMES

The distinction between sentences, images, and events is obviously a rough one, and ultimately melts away. The sentences (like "You are the light of the world") are all more or less imagistic and often depend to some degree on their event-context. The images (like manna appearing daily to nourish the wandering Jews) gain their meaning in part from their prior embeddedness in a verbal and event-context. The events (like Krishna appearing to Arjuna in the Gita) are mediated to us through images and words. Still, in practice there is a different entry point to these three kinds of meditations.

Meditations that focus on a sentence tend to involve us in many more words and conceptual understandings as we begin to focus on them. They can become too "heady," too abstract, if not pursued to their core. They become meditations worthy of the name only when they dissolve into feeling-experiences—feelings, mind you, not emotions. Their great advantage is that, by slowly building their significance through our work of thinking, when we let go of words these meditations help us to stay within the zone of the theme's meaning more precisely than with the other kinds of starting points.

Meditations that focus on an image have the advantage that they begin with something that evokes feeling. A picture, as it is often said, is worth a thousand words. The image invites us to identify with it, to become it, in a way that the sentence does not, initially. For image meditation, too, we want the feeling that it evokes to carry us without our being disturbed by the initial theme. It is harder for this feeling, however, to lead into an articulated logos-sphere for most beginners, for whom it is very likely to dissipate into vagueness or distractions.

Events or stories as meditative themes have some of the advantages and dangers of both the earlier forms, as well as features of their own. They lead us, through a sequence of resonant images, into an entrainment in the theme. They have the quality of not settling into a static form, but obviously, right from the start, the themes exist within the process of telling or picturing them; they do not exist at any final moment or in any kind of moral. The story as a whole does not exist at any fixed time, for example at its close; rather, it unrolls throughout its reception.

Objects of the natural world, such as leaves, landscapes, shells, stones, animals, clouds, and so on, can very well become primary themes of meditation. They will hardly unlock their secrets unless we begin to approach them through previously schooled and concentrated thinking and feeling, with the same attention to the play of distractions required by other kinds of meditation. Unlike meditative sentences, natural objects have no meaning for ordinary consciousness, so we have to leap to their significance in a different way. In the case of a meditative sentence, we grow intimate with the theme through an intensification of normal thinking. In the case of meditative perception, we grow intimate with the theme through a reversal of the feeling-will so that it comes toward us from the "object." This has nothing to do with normal thinking about the object. More can be read about meditative perception in my *Stairway of Surprise* or in Georg Kühlewind's *Education of the Senses*.

The theme in its origin, an aspect of the light, is not any one element of everyday consciousness, but all of them at once, and none of them, and much more. It is actually neither inner nor outer, neither visual nor auditory nor conceptual, but stems from the same source as all of these. As Rilke put it, in a kind of command to the meditant:

> Be, in this night of overabundance,
> The magic power at the intersection of your senses,
> The sense of their unusual encounter.

Themes are runways, entry points, portals. For one person, or at one moment, an apparently abstract theme may be the way through to intensity of being; for that person, or another, or at another moment, an apparently imagistic theme or perceptual object may be the way through. It is good to experiment with all types of themes, especially, perhaps, those that seem hard or wrong for you at first. Your steady gaze will make them open.

> You need not leave your room. Remain sitting at your table and listen. You need not even listen, simply wait, just learn to become quiet, and still, and solitary. The world will freely offer itself to you to be unmasked. It has no choice; it will roll in ecstasy at your feet. (Franz Kafka)

DANCE OF THE SEVEN VEILS

As Kühlewind emphasizes, every level of understanding depends on renunciation of a previous level. To understand a word, I must already understand the letters of which it is composed and then release my tight fixation on the letters to focus on the word as a whole. To understand a sentence, I have to release my tight hold on the individual words. To understand a paragraph or larger unit of writing, I must both understand and release the separate sentences.

Behind the initial, denotative meaning of a meditative sentence or image or natural object, there lie other meanings toward which I can project my intuitive sensing. This means letting go of the sentence, image, or object, while staying on track with its gesture or staying within its neighborhood of meaning. If I succeed in feeling the next-higher meaning or meanings, these cannot necessarily be expressed with any other words than those of the initial meditation sentence, for example; yet, now this sentence has power and life it never had before.

The process does not end here. Any attained meaning can be renounced in favor of a still higher or livelier, more encompassing meaning that lies behind it.

Such spatial terminology ("higher," "behind," "below," "above") may be misleading. At times, for instance, the new range of meanings we experience can seem to be "in front of" the former meaning, not hidden behind it but, on the contrary, hidden only by virtue of being too obvious to see. As we suggested above, compared with our normal thinking, meditation brings us to more immediate, in fact less mysterious meanings. It reveals that our normal perceptual world (the things that seem to be around us), and our normal conceptual world (the meanings that seem to be within us), and our normal feeling world (the emotions that seem to enliven us), are all of them unnecessarily obscure and complicated. Our new sense of things is clear, evident, generous, and free.

To get there, we do have to sacrifice something (that is, everything), since we must abandon our sense of certainty. Instead of giving us a rock-solid basis from which to proceed, meditation unsettles our initial feeling that we know what's going on, for instance, with the theme. It can bring a profound sense of groundedness and participation, but not in a way that flatters our hankering after easy certainty. On the way to the ground, we may have to go through immeasurable groundlessness.

There are not seven veils, then, but an infinite number. Every achieved understanding of the theme is both a fulfillment and an impediment. At every level, the theme itself hides its deeper nature. It is up to us to create and receive the theme's ever more intimate possibilities.

LOVE

Why meditate if the result is chilly?

It is certainly a sign that something is wrong if our meditations become repetitive, or coldly abstract, or if the discussions about them become acrimonious. Spiritual practice of the kind described in this book begins in earnest playfulness; it ends in love.

The love in question is not quite everyday love, though of the same universal source. It is specifically a love that can unite two or more people in spite of their not really liking each other, in spite of many personal differences. It comes with an aroma of freedom, easiness, availability, openhandedness, which is the natural result of our immersion in the theme.

Let us build a sketch, step by step, of the progress of love through meditation. Here then, as the first step, is the human being as a partially fixed form:

U

The "U" in its solid-line base and walls represents the stable identity, the "body" of the person. This means a physical body, a body of habits, the identity as man or woman, the prejudices of all kinds, the likes and dislikes. The body includes the body of formative forces, the body of our mental and emotional responses, and the body of our language and our relationships as already known. Only at the top of the "U" is there an opening. This represents the partial openness of each of us—open to new ideas, new people, new experiences, capable of forgiveness and other forms of creativity. When our sense of self resides firmly in the center of the "U," we identify with our bodies. As we concentrate in meditation, or on anything really, we rise a bit within the "U," or even rise completely outside the "U" into the open air above.

Now here are two people meeting under ordinary circumstances:

$$U <> U$$

If they relate to each other from out of their fixed formedness, they will like or dislike each other, understand each other as husks, and have a normal relationship. What they are perceiving about each other is only their "bodies"—with which they totally identify.

If, however, they are both concentrating or meditating, they each leave their realm of certainty, fixity, familiarity. They lift out of their many bodies and into the open air of intuition above them. Then, two things happen. First, they become more available to the ideas or intuitions streaming down to them from out of the open. This corresponds to what I have been calling vertical peace. Second, they are in fact less separate and relate to one another now within that zone of openness—horizontal peace:

The relationship to one another is "above" the experience of fixed forms. We no longer meet as husk to husk, but as openness-to-openness.

The husks, too, can now be appreciated for what they are: miraculous preconditions for the very act of overcoming them that is love.

The kind of love attained through meditation is an "after-everything love." It is as if after a profound shared tragedy, or after great physical exertion, or after an argument and forgiveness. It has the quality of the blissful calm after the storm, though it can be exciting in its own right as well. It is a love that points to the reality of the other person as other, yet in a shared mutual space with oneself. It says not only "I AM," but also "YOU ARE."

Loving the Husks

We do not grow in love by ignoring our differences, ignoring our husks, or abandoning our boundaries altogether. We grow precisely by witnessing them within our openness to the whole situation at hand. This too I learned at Harlem Hospital, where for nine years I was the Chief Psychologist in Pediatric AIDS. I was one of just a few white clinicians in an African-American institution. What I found over and over was that my whiteness came between me and other members of the team, as well as between me and patients, as far more of a problem when it went unacknowledged. When either I or my African-American colleagues brought up the fact of our difference, conversation invariably went better.

In "spiritual" groups there is a great danger of pseudo-similarity. People want to affiliate, don't want to stick out, and we can end up in a mutually limiting caress of prejudices. We may too strenuously avoid any acknowledgment of differences, ignorances, mistakes. We sometimes want already to be so above the level of husks and bodies that we live in a pseudo-world of homogenized unity, nodding too often and taking a stand too rarely. We could celebrate our differences, rather than try to annihilate them.

In this same style of acknowledging what is really going on, we can understand John's reference to the healing power of admitting to any missteps or mistakes (1 John 1:8–10):

> If we say that we have not made a mistake, we deceive ourselves, and the truth is not in us. If we admit our mistakes, he is faithful and just to forgive us these mistakes and to cleanse us from all unrighteousness. If we say that we have made no mistakes, we make him a liar, and his word is not in us.

Here I translate *hamartia* as "mistake" rather than as "sin." The original Greek term is actually from archery, and it means "missing the mark." It is not a moral condemnation.

As long as we still defend our rightness, our position, our mistakes, we remain separate and unfruitful. If we can acknowledge our poor aim, our partiality, our limitedness, it both is the result of, and results in, freedom within these very limitations. The person who can admit he or she is angry, for example, already has the ability to be free of the anger. The person who has to deny his or her anger, jealousy, fear (unfortunately we must add "etc.") is the person completely caught in it.

During meditative practice, we turn aside from our various husks, as well as from any self-evaluation, but this is not a suppression or denial. Rather, immersion in the meditative theme makes us discover that we are citizens of that open space in which we can more lightly understand our separateness. This in turn leads to a better meditation the next time, which may lead to a clearer sense of still more of one's limitations and missteps, and also the beauty of our very separateness. Steiner referred to the same process under the heading of "the guardian of the threshold."

THE SPEAKING WORLD

A client in psychotherapy was noticing how closely her current behavior resembled her early reactions to childhood trauma. She felt what she called a "corridor" of continuous maladaptive habits and feelings from her childhood abuse right through to her current problematic marriage. The amazing thing was that, while she described this continuity, she was smiling. I asked why.

"Oh," she said, "it's not because of a nice thought. These are horrible things. But just the seeing of it is good."

It spoke to her. As Nietzsche said, "What signifies, delights." This is what my client experienced. There is goodness, even pleasure, in any meaning whatsoever, even in the most painful memory. Not the continuity of maladaptive behavior was good, but her sense that the course of her life was a word, a meaning. Her realizing it was good.

With the gaze of the soul habitually and intentionally aimed at significance, we can open ourselves more and more completely in meditation, unconcerned that we will be assaulted by outer or inward foes. We are on the hunt for the meaningful, untroubled by the unmeaningful.

Logos is a term for the power of meaning that lies both at the base of our minds now and of the world we normally see as outside us and other than us. "What became [the world] was life in him [in the logos]," according to the Gospel of John, "and the life was the light of men." In other words, one single quality (called "life" here) makes up both our consciousness and the world of which we are conscious. "We have seen," writes the young Rudolf Steiner in his doctoral dissertation *Truth and Science,* "that the essence of the world lives itself out in our knowing." The Logos orientation of the meditative path described here means that we are always moving into greater understanding, and that the world is becoming more meaningful around us. This has nothing to do with Christianity as opposed to other traditions: they are all logos-oriented in their origin.

In Judaism, this orientation is obvious from numerous examples, notably that the first act of creation was one of speech, "And God said, 'Let there be light.'" It continues through the Tower of Babel, where ambition replaced meaning for the builders, so that they lost the power of understanding and separated into different language groups. It persists through Moses, who was forbidden to enter the Holy Land because he used power-magic, rather than word-magic, to bring water from the rock.

In the same way, again in Goethe's *Faust,* we notice that Mephistopheles arises out of his poodle-form into the devil's form just when Faust mistranslates John's statement, "In the beginning was the Word," as, "In the beginning was the Deed." This power orientation brings ill consequences for Faust, just as it did for Moses.

Again, in the Zen tradition, the koans or "public cases" are dialogic in many ways. On the one hand, they are accounts of dialogues between masters and disciples. Then, too, those dialogues usually took place in front of monks who witnessed it. The koan is later given as a spiritual task, or problem, by a master to a student. From first to last, the koan is about the fact of addressing. "Can you speak a true word?" asks a master in one such story, but his interlocutor has nothing to say. The fact that we can address one another, if we really can address one another, carries within it all that we need to know.

Self-Meaning

Every understanding is non-dual. For a split second, you become whatever you understand and only later, though merely a nanosecond later, you wake up to the thing understood, which now seems separate from you.

The original non-dual moment is approached and made to linger in the act of meditation. We experience it by noticing that our very act of focusing on the theme becomes indistinguishable from the theme itself. This can happen with any high theme if we take it seriously enough. In a meditation on the phrase "I am the light of the world," for example, our effort in seeking the light of the world becomes itself that light, confirming the theme. In a meditation on "Every moment is a little door through which the messiah could enter," our inquiry itself becomes such a moment, such a door, and such a messiah.

To put it another way, a meditative sentence is precisely a sentence that can mean itself, rather than indicate something outside itself. Normally, a sentence does the latter. A sentence like "There is salt on the table already" conveys a meaning that is not about the sentence or about the act of saying it. It is about the salt and the table. But meditative sentences, or their thinking or utterance, become examples of whatever they describe. It has been pointed out that the most self-referential words are "I" and "word," and both words implicate their own speaking. Only I can say "I" while using it to mean myself. The utterance of "word" always demonstrates what it describes. It may be that, ultimately, every word, sentence, and phenomenon can be understood to mean itself, in this way, rather than to stand outside reality and describe it from afar.

We can easily sense self-meaning in the case of perceptual meditation. A rock, a shell, a tree, very obviously do not "mean" anything else, anything other than themselves. The trick is to deepen our perception of them to the point where they become more meanings than objects. What they mean can be only their own nature. As Gerard Manley Hopkins put it in "As kingfishers catch fire, dragonflies dráw flále":

> Each mortal thing does one thing and the same:
> Deals out that being indoors each one dwells;
> Selves—goes itself; *myself* it speaks and spells,
> Crying *Whát I do is me: for that I came.*

Self-meaning is closely related to ineffability. Most descriptions of spiritual activity never give a content of the experience directly. They describe everything around it—the setting, the techniques, the effects— just not the experience itself. This is because spiritual experience cannot be described, even if it included words to some degree. The experience meant itself alone and uniquely. Any language that would attempt to reproduce it, from the outside, could only mis-describe it. When Robert Frost was asked what was meant by one of his poems, he replied, "Do you want me to say it again in worse language?" In the description of the day of Pentecost, for example, with the first appearance of the Holy Spirit among a group of self-directed meditants, the preamble and the reception of the experience are given, but the heart of what they were going through is left masterfully blank.

Being

From one angle, as we have noted, the purpose of meditation is just to exist more intensively. We realize our existence, both in the sense that we become aware of it and in the sense that we make it a reality. These two apparently distinct kinds of realization become a single procedure in meditative realization alone.

"Why is there something rather than nothing?" asked Martin Heidegger. This marveling at the fact of existence mostly arrives unsought, if it is more than an abstract inquiry, and it trails generosity, joy and understanding in its wake. We feel, in this inquiry, not that we have mastered new information, or that we are in possession of anything at all, but only that we are living now at a more resonant pitch of being. We feel, at such moments, that this life is real, shockingly real, and always was, and brims with possibility. It may not be another reality that comes into view, but the reality of this reality. The world, as Kafka and Steiner both mentioned, is not an illusion: only our normal take on it is illusion. At moments of realization, we see how very existent this world is.

I was leading a group and a woman began to discuss her meditation. "Sometimes," she said, "after a meditation or during it or just walking along the corridor of my office building, I realize, 'I exist.' And that is everything, and incredible, and beautiful. 'I exist.'"

THE LORD

When the scrolls of the Torah are read out loud in a synagogue, a certain word is pronounced over and over. This word is *adonai,* which means literally "my lord," but is translated most often as "the Lord." In many translations it is written all capitals, as "the LORD."

Though we may say *adonai,* and though the translations into English mostly say "the LORD," this is not what is written in Hebrew in the Torah. At that point in the text, the actual written letters are *Yod Heh Vav Heh,* or in English letters, *YHWH.* When transliterated and given vowels (which do not appear in the Hebrew and are really just a guess), it is written *Yahweh* or *Jehovah.*

Now, *YHWH* does not mean "lord" or "my lord," or anything of the kind. Rather, this four-letter term or "tetragrammaton" was the sacred, unpronounceable name of God, and *adonai* is routinely spoken in its place out of a kind of holy awe or respect. In the traditional context, no one ever pronounces these letters or knows how. At times, the reader will say *ha shem* instead of *adonai,* which means "the name" instead of "my lord." But *YHWH,* the name of God, remains unpronounced and untranslated by these or other substitutions. It means neither name nor lord.

So those hundreds or thousands of references to "the Lord" or to "God's name" in the Bible—the Lord who creates the world, for example, or tells Isaiah what to preach, or who is called "my shepherd" in the Twenty-third Psalm—all refer to this untranslated term, *YHWH.*

What then, you might ask at last, does this term *YHWH* mean? Would this not seem to be important, since it is appealed to over and over as the authority behind the whole of the Jewish, Christian, and Islamic traditions? What is this name of God, and what does it tell us, if it means anything? What would it do for us not to take this name in vain, as the Third Commandment enjoins us, but actually to know what it is all about?

Unfortunately, historical linguists of ancient Hebrew are not exactly sure what *YHWH* means. However, there is a broad agreement that it is some form of the verb *to be*. It may be the infinitive.

Oh.

So all those invocations of "the Lord" or "the LORD" become much more meaningful and suggestive and, you might say, existential. "Being is my shepherd; how could I have a desire?"—might then be a more sense-specific translation of the opening to the Twenty-third Psalm. The same Psalm ends with the hope: "I will dwell in the house of Being forever." "Behold the handmaid of Being," says Mary at the annunciation. "Blessed is he who comes in the name of Being," declares the One-Hundred-Eighteenth Psalm. With this understanding, the patriarchy is gone, and the primordial fact of existence is known both as original motivator and as current initiator of all that is good. When Jesus addresses God and says he has declared God's name while on Earth, we can see this as not a trivial matter or a question of announcing some doctrinal allegiance, but as the fundamental teaching Jesus had to offer. He declared how to be at all.

Let us return for a moment to the validity of replacing this term, *YHWH,* with a circumlocution like "the Lord." The tradition is wise to do so, even if harm has come from choosing "the Lord" with its patriarchal connotations, and from forgetting that there is such an operation of replacement in the first place. We could easily say, "I exist," or,

"You exist," or, "The world is," a thousand times and all the more miss the sacred, astonishing quality of this being, the generative, bursting-open potential that is every instant. By saying "the Lord," we fruitfully refuse to kill the mystery of being. Lao Tze opens his masterpiece about the Way precisely with the statement: "The Tao that can be named is not the eternal Tao." What cannot be named, obviously, belongs to no particular religion. To recover the all-encompassing promise of the Name, then, we need far more than an accurate translation. We need a meditative path.

SHAMELESSNESS

The best hint in the Bible about meditation comes in the Gospel of Luke (11:5–13). The disciples had been asking for instruction, and they received the Lord's Prayer and the advice "seek and ye shall find." However, between these two famous passages lies another, less familiar one that contains a tiny parable. God the Father is likened to a man who has gone to sleep, and the meditant, or praying soul, is compared to a friend who comes to wake him, knocking on his door to ask for bread. The text says that God will not give him bread out of love but because of the person's *shamelessness* in knocking.

This is the key. The whole story began, after all, with Adam and Eve hiding in shame from God's presence (Genesis 3:8–10). The advice here about shamelessness signals the end of our alienation from the ground of being. Our own impulse in meditation or prayer, our asking with the shamelessness that holds nothing back, makes it possible for God to give us his gifts.

The parable refers to those gifts as "breads." The one knocking is asking specifically for three of them. This refers to three higher levels of "I AM" experience, which Steiner calls *spirit self, life spirit,* and *spirit body.* Bread, after all, is the pervasive symbol for the "I AM" of the Logos. *Bethlehem* in Hebrew means "House of Bread." The baby is laid in a manger, or feed trough. The Logos later speaks the equivalence of terms explicitly: "I AM: the bread that came down from heaven" (John 6:41).

In the parable, these higher selves, or breads, are begged from God, not for the sake of the praying soul but for the sake of someone else, a friend who has come "out of the Way." In other words, we do not seek the fruits of meditation for ourselves alone; we can ask for them shamelessly precisely because we are part of a larger whole, a community of mutual giving, in which we pass on that which we receive.

FROM EMOTION TO FEELING

What keeps us from wonder at existence today is above all our self-oriented emotional life. Our everyday emotions, which involve agitation of the physical body, mostly inform us only about ourselves. They are not feelings, since they tell us nothing about the world around us or about other people. We have forgotten that there could be such feelings—feelings of young children for the grammar of their mother tongue, for example.

Adult-style emotion in our time is sticky. It tends to linger. Just this feature is notably absent in small children. Even when they have tears, the tears suddenly dry up. The involution of feeling, such that attention sticks to it, has not yet taken place. Babies and toddlers have no sentimentality, do not hold a grudge, are never in a bad mood that lasts for a whole day, and are not wistful. They neither have a good self-image nor a poor one, and just that is health.

Instead of our kind of lingering, self-involved, adult emotions, small children have an extraordinarily intelligent capacity to feel the world around them. They feel through to the grammatical structures of the language spoken to them, but also to the qualities of the silence that their family exemplifies. They sense, often much more accurately than adults, the mood and intent of those near to them. Rather than emotions, which make a lot of inward commotion within and about ourselves, they do actually have feelings worthy of the name, feelings that feel the reality of the world.

For adults, a return to something like the freshness, mobility, and alertness of childhood feeling can be both a helpful precondition for, and a blessed result of, meditative practice. For it is always ultimately a feeling, a love, by which we know the meditative theme. This love can be developed as an intentional power, like thinking. To do so, we need to turn our emotions into feelings. We need to turn inside out.

Here is Novalis, the early Romantic era German poet and philosopher, on the subject of feeling:

> Does he (the human being) only learn to feel once? This most heavenly, this most natural of all senses he still knows only slightly. Through feeling, the ancient, longed-for age could return. The element of feeling is an inner light that refracts into more beautiful, more powerful colors. Then the starry constellations would arise within him, he would learn to feel the whole world more clearly and more variegatedly than the

eye now shows him limits and surfaces. He would be master
of an endless play, and forget all foolish strivings in an eternal,
self-nourishing, and ever-increasing pleasure. Thinking is only
a dream of feeling, a pale-gray, weak life.

It was one of the great insights of the Romantic era, of which Novalis
was a leading light, that emotions are inherently neither subjective nor
selfish, but only appear so in their normal, fallen form. Poets and thinkers
of this time recognized that we can develop our feeling-attentiveness by
turning it toward worthy objects in a certain way. This both gives us the
"object" more intimately, and changes us in the act of viewing. Novalis's
close contemporary in England, the young William Wordsworth, was
writing about how to ennoble the emotions in "Tintern Abbey," where he
calls them "affections." This purification or transformation takes place
precisely as we allow the emotions to be active although the body, normally agitated in emotional experience, is left quiet:

> ...the affections gently lead us on
> until the breath of this corporeal frame,
> and even the motion of our human blood
> almost suspended, we are laid asleep
> in body and become a living soul,
> while with an eye made quiet by the power
> of harmony, and the deep power of joy,
> we see into the life of things.

Wordsworth's young colleague John Keats put the issue of emotions
versus feelings in a more therapeutic way. He counseled specifically against

medication for depression, in his "Ode on Melancholy," and suggested that the dark feeling of melancholy could instead become perceptive. Melancholy, and by extension the other emotions, is for Keats a power of perception turned inward on one's self. It can be turned outward again:

> No, no! go not to Lethe, neither twist
> Wolf's-bane, tight-rooted, for its poisonous wine;
> Nor suffer thy pale forehead to be kiss'd
> By nightshade, ruby grape of Proserpine;
> . . . .
> But when the melancholy fit shall fall
> . . . .
> Then glut thy sorrow on the morning rose,
> Or on the rainbow of the salt sand-wave,
> Or on the wealth of globed peonies . . .

In part two, we will look at some practical steps to make this move from emotion to feeling so passionately counseled by the Romantics.

DISTRACTIONS

Anything that isn't the theme is a distraction.

There are so many kinds of distractions, and they can bewitch us both by their compelling subject matter and by their very variety. We are distracted by physical sensations of all kinds, including pain in the body, the sound of a bird or a car outside, and so on. Memories present distractions, even the memory of previous encounters with the theme. As memory it is not our current immersion in the theme. We are distracted by plans, by projects, by preoccupations. We are distracted by doubt and drowsiness. We are distracted by our normal social awareness of the other meditants in the room with us. We are distracted by the idea that we may later report on our meditation. There are, in fact, innumerable distractions—really, the whole world is a distraction.

The solution to distraction is always the same: Back to the theme! That's the whole story. As soon as you notice that your mind has wandered, you gently, smilingly, return to the theme.

All deviations from the theme have the same value, which is nil. It is unwise, in meditation, to analyze why your mind wandered or where it wandered. This actually represents succumbing to the distraction. Rather, the power of meditation increases as you leave the distraction and re-present yourself to your theme. Nevertheless, it is worth noticing after a meditation, as you think back on its course, that distractions tend to be about yourself, and they tend to be familiar in content and style. In other words, they are selfish and uncreative.

There is a key point that may sound theoretical, but that becomes very practical when you call it up in response to noticing that the mind has wandered. It is this: the whole mind is always entirely dedicated. It may not be available to your conscious control, but the whole of your mental/emotional/spiritual energies or forces, the whole of who you are, is always somewhere. So in a wider sense there is no possibility of distraction. The mind is dedicated, involved, concentrated, but in pieces. It is not our goal to get rid of the distractions, exactly. We recognize that the power of the mind is present in them. It is rather a matter of gathering the disparate investments of attention, each of which is dedicated or absorbed, back into one clear, intentional beam. We can recall that "conscience," like "conscious," comes from the Latin for "knowing together." When all the parts of yourself know together, then you are conscious and your conscience is active. It becomes clear that the practice of meditation leads both to a cognitive and a moral progress. But this takes doing.

Once, a woman entering our meditation on some high and beautiful theme, with wholehearted devotion, found that what came to her instead of any grand revelation, as if by way of hostile contrast, was her history of sexual abuse. It presented itself unmistakably and unavoidably to her mind, obscuring the theme, no matter which way she turned. She was overwhelmed with loss, fear, anger, and emptiness. Finally, she had to run from the room, filled with anguish. This took place during a two-day workshop, and she allowed herself to take a walk for an hour, returning only when she felt ready. On rejoining us, she again gave herself wholeheartedly to the group work. In other words, she had to go through the self-encounter brought on by meditation and be merciful with herself as it became too much for her. She did not pretend she could focus when she simply couldn't. Then, after gathering herself, she could face the theme afresh, having allowed some of the straw of who she was to be burned up by the fire of the approaching truth.

WORTHINESS

A special distraction that troubles many practitioners is the feeling of worthlessness. Who am I to be privileged to taste this high theme?, we may ask ourselves at times. I am unworthy. I cannot be here, enjoying this beauty. News from heaven could come only to someone more senior, someone more practiced, someone without my flaws and faults, someone holier.

With this particular distraction, as with all distractions, it is important to note that, however humble or trenchant it may sound, it is not the theme. As such, it is technically *self-ish,* being oriented toward one's own person. It represents a falling-away from immersive attention to the theme, and while it may be a good question to ponder at some other time, we will only grow more able to address it if, for the time of the meditation, we let the theme be all in all.

Low self-esteem, after all, cannot be countered by high self-esteem. I mentioned seeing kindergarten children so absorbed in listening to a fairy tale that they drool and don't even notice they are drooling. That is the healthy, invisible self-esteem: the person is so secure that she has no regard for herself. In adulthood, the secure equivalent is the I AM experience that comes from selfless attention.

The distraction of unworthiness is closely related to the "too good to be true" problem. We are overly familiar with bad, even bitter news. Failure, death, betrayal, destruction, hatred—this is the kind of thing that seems real. We almost have no available mindset for good news. If there were any joy, delight, unclouded happiness, any amazing good fortune, any good at all that had a chance against the evil in the world, who is allowed to know it or assert it? The unspoken feeling seems to be: good news is always false, or at least cannot come to me.

The traditional problem of theodicy was how to justify that evil exists when there is also supposed to be a benevolent, omnipotent God as creator and witness. The emphasis was on the scandalous fact of evil. That was the shocking news that demanded justification. The problem we find in contemporary meditation is almost the opposite: how to accept a wonderful meditative claim, a joyous result, or a splendid truth about the world, when we know that we ourselves, and the world around us, are so full of troubles. If this kind of difficulty comes up during meditation, as we have said, we need only set it aside and return to the theme. An actual answer to the question of worthiness and the question of "too good to be true" could come as the result of a specific meditation undertaken on a different occasion. A suitable meditation on this theme might be: "What is man, that thou art mindful of him?" (Psalm 8:4)

The Normal, Failed Act of Attention

Ideally, we would choose a theme and think it, delving deeper and deeper into it, letting it reveal its depths to us, and become self-forgetfully one with it. Enlivened thinking would lead without transition to cognitive feeling, its mother, and from this to still deeper reaches of understanding in which, so to say, the will is reversed and the theme understands us.

This entire course of events does in fact happen, but only for micro-moments, mostly unnoticed, with any act of attention no matter how slight. Ideally, again, we would stay with the theme for whatever length of time we had set ourselves, or—and this would be the best case—until the inwardly felt right moment to leave it.

Yet our normal acts of attention do not feel like this. They are failures in the sense that we get distracted well before any length of time we have set ourselves to stay concentrated, and also long before we have adequately dealt with our chosen theme. The drama of our chronically distracted mind, which can be very confusing inwardly, gets a bit clearer if we separate it out schematically into four phases and consider their peculiarities.

1. **Focus:** You choose a focus, a theme—whether this is the breath or a meditative sentence or what have you. By a capacity you did not invent and cannot wholly eradicate, it is given to you to choose such a focus and to dive into it. Sometimes the mind is so confused, in pain, or tattered, that it may seem that you cannot focus at all. But you never quite lose the ability to choose your focus at least for an instant at a time.

2. **Wander to Distraction:** Somehow, as if falling prey to a siren song, in a kind of dream, you are lured away into distractions, associations, reveries, confusion, doubt. You wander from the theme. You are no longer with "God is light," but a million miles away. You are mulling over some offense given you by a relative or colleague. You are embarrassed by your burbling stomach. The wandering, the distraction, may seem to lie very close to the theme in some sense, yet it still separates you from the theme decisively. For example, you wander into doubt as to whether this is the right theme, or you wander into self-evaluation of your meditation, or you simply remain in theoretical manipulations of the theme without allowing it to deepen.

3. **Wake Up:** Somehow, you wake up to the fact of having wandered. There you were wandering near or far, and suddenly you notice that you have left the theme. This is a point of clarity in the mind, often swiftly followed by self-criticism, which is of course no help. The

moment of "wake-up" is a good moment to be gentle with yourself, as you are given a fresh possibility. All too often, though, you fall right back into wandering, as if you had been aroused briefly from sleep only to sink back again.

4. **Refocus:** Instead of continuing the topic of the distraction, you remember the original theme and decide to take up again the project you had unwittingly abandoned. It is not simply a given that you will return to the theme. You must choose to do so, and it often feels as if this choice is harder than the original choice of the theme. It is like swimming to shore against an outgoing tide.

Notice that steps 1 (Focus) and 4 (Refocus) are both decidedly chosen by you. If you don't choose them, they don't come about. By contrast, steps 2 (Wander to Distraction) and 3 (Wake Up) are not chosen. No one chooses to wander: if we did, this would not be wandering but the conscious choice of a new theme. And no one chooses to wake up: to do so, one would already have to be awake.

It is an unconscious force in us that seems to drug us to sleep and drag us to distraction so that we wander from the theme. And it is another, quite different unconscious force in us that later seems to slap us awake and make us face the fact that we have wandered. Both processes happen outside our awareness: we have already wandered by the time we notice we are wandering; we have already woken up by the time we notice that we have awakened.

These two unconscious forces have very different aims. The force that makes us wander is actively hostile to the project of focus. It seduces us away. It has endless ammunition for the task, using memory, sleepiness, doubt, fear, anticipation, physical sensation, and every element of the universe to substitute for the theme.

The force that makes us wake up, by contrast, is not so much friendly to focus as it is friendly to freedom. It never forces us to refocus, but presents us only with the situation we have gotten into and silently poses the question of what we will do next. It can be an uncomfortable moment in several ways, a tug of conscience, an annoying sense of a task undone. It is a pivotal point. At times, we can be acutely aware of feeling both the desire to let go and continue wandering, and also the desire to re-immerse in the theme. The choice is ours.

Of course, this whole drama is not a "failure" exactly, as I suggested in the title of this section, but simply the real life of the mind as it develops its capacity to pay attention. There is no point in regretting distractions or in blaming ourselves. There is just the theme, waiting there for us to remember and embrace it.

As concentration deepens, we wander less frequently away from our immersion in the theme, and also we go less far off in each spell of wandering. At times, the only remaining distraction is our very awareness of what has just come into consciousness, a kind of inner confirmation or affirmation of what we have just thought, just realized, just felt. But this slight reflection, this slight heaving away from the theme to check on it or notice ourselves, can itself also be renounced, at least for certain periods, so that the energy of self-awareness it represents is plowed back into the theme itself, and we do no more onlooking from without.

Peace Again

If we were to meditate the passage from the Gospel of John about leaving us with his peace, we would first discuss and ponder its meanings. In a group, this is a matter for voluntary and playful open discussion, complete with crosstalk, interruptions, quotations, references, memories about events in one's life that illustrate some aspect of the theme, and so on. For purposes of this section, I just want to mention some of the perspectives that make the theme central for an understanding of group meditation in general.

"Peace I leave unto you. . . ."

This peace is being left with us even though Jesus prepares to leave earthly incarnation in his then form. It was all around him like a garment, it is shed or left behind with us as he leaves. The physical form will go; the peace he brought will stay. The implication is that by being incarnate in a human form, Christ changed the structure of what it is to be human altogether, and so left as a permanent condition of human being that we all have access, as never before, to the open heavens. But how exactly did his example make it the case that peace is "left" here? What is it about that incarnation that might have changed the openness or closedness of all people, not just those who knew him?

". . . my peace I give you. . . ."

"My" peace indicates that it is not some generic peace, but it also does not mean a peace Jesus owns. It is the peace he is himself: the peace that is the Word. This is why, after first saying that he leaves peace, he now emphasizes that he is giving "his" peace.

As a gift, the peace mentioned here reminds us both of the "gifts of the Holy Spirit," and also of the giftedness of all our capacities. Peace is itself the Holy Spirit—the all-encompassing gift making possible any particular spiritual gifts. We could take this from another angle and say that therefore we ourselves can now be words spoken from heaven. The gift of peace makes this embeddedness possible.

"... not as the world gives. . . . "

The world gives things that seem solid but pass soon enough, for example with our deaths. Things like this include money, power, fame, popularity, sensual pleasure. But this category also includes all fixed ideas, "world views," cosmologies, religious dogmas of all kinds. That is all given as the world gives. Anything we cling to, anything we think will guarantee good times for us—anything at all, then, in normal consciousness, is stuff that we receive "as the world gives."

We have a model for the very different way the peace in question is being given. For with all our basic capacities, for example musical talent, or the ability to think or speak, we do nothing to deserve them or obtain them. They come, not as objects, but as potentials. In fact, this was the original meaning of the word *gift* in English—not a thing, but a talent. Capacities have no exact content, but their content is always changing and open for revision. In a way, they are nothing, yet as powerful potentials they are much stronger than any specific and determined thing. We can ask, with regard to all the basic capacities: Where do they come from? Who invented them? What kind of mind could create them or give them? If we let them, such questions bring us to the edge of the known world or even a smidgen beyond it. By saying, "not as the world gives," Christ is saying that he gives his peace as a capacity. Peace is not something we can ever have. It is something for us to do and be.

A gift in the everyday world enriches an already-existing self. You already have many possessions that enrich you, and here comes another possession. You keep the possession until you give it away, lose it, sell it, die, or find that it has decayed. But the gift of peace requires for its reception a radically different gesture. It requires that you give yourself utterly, and each time. It is no help here to have a belief system or to belong to an organization. Rather, each time you meditate you receive peace in the measure that you give yourself up to the meditative theme.

THE ANGLE OF INCIDENCE

We always, necessarily, aim at the meditative theme from a particular angle, from out of our own habits of thought, for example. Cultural considerations also come into play. Then there is the specific culture of the group, and the style and perhaps the all-too-familiar insights of the group leader. All these elements give us a characteristic slant on the theme. Our discussion and subsequent pondering will tend to reflect this slant, these predispositions. Also, of course we want to "have" something from the meditation, while the gesture of possession kills all higher knowing:

> He who binds to himself a joy
> Doth the winged life destroy
> He who kisses joy as it flies
> Lives in Eternitys sun rise (WILLIAM BLAKE)

As concentration intensifies, the inadequacy of what we have already thought and known becomes apparent. Previous conceptions grow brittle or dissolve. It is not simply that we drop old views and gain new insights of a familiar sort. Rather, the direction, the bent, the angle of incidence of the new understandings is always surprising. This does not arrive from who we think we are, and from what we think the universe is about: it arrives from who we really are, and from what the universe is really about. And that undoes us.

It is as if the truth of the theme ambushes us. We were marching along unawares, dutifully thinking about the theme, with some interruptions perhaps, when out of nowhere the theme pops out in a new guise, demands everything we've got at knife point, then showers us with petals.

ACCESS

Whatever we may choose to meditate on, we must have some access to it through ordinary consciousness before we begin to meditate. We choose a theme from a language we know, for example.

But we do not choose just any theme. We pick a theme that we suspect has a high source. It has an aroma of Heaven-on-Earth. We sense that whoever wrote or made it was operating from our true home.

We can make such selections with some accuracy because we are never completely cut off from the sources of intuition. We already possess an almost-ignorable access to the place to which we seek entry; somehow we are already resident there. Ordinary consciousness is itself continually fueled by its own higher sources, or it would not be consciousness at all. Our initial choice of a meditation theme is informed from these sources, and meditation consists in a fuller expression of their initial hinting, a widening of access. At some point we can realize what the medieval mystic Meister Eckhart announced—that "the eye by which I see God is the eye by which God sees me."

In a group, part of the thrashing-through or hashing-out phase may be the selection of the exact passage or image to focus on. It is good if a preponderance of the group feels, "Yes, we can meditate this one. There is gold hidden here." It can take some time for the group to align and come into resonance with the theme to be sought. We ready ourselves, even through disagreement, to be open and gathered toward the theme.

Goethe pointed to this prior affinity between what we seek and how we seek it:

> If the eye were not sun-like,
> how could it see the Sun?
> If God's own power were not in us,
> how could divinity delight us?

The group that meditates makes it possible to touch on this shared access by the overcoming of the disparity, the divergences of the group. As the discussion progresses, we become not of one mind, but of like mind, and our focus on the theme opens us to a super-individual realm where our differences do not dissolve and yet we sup at a common spiritual table. That is why Goethe's observations are couched in the first-person plural.

When one of his jailers asked the early Quaker leader George Fox about how to know Scripture, he answered, "By the same spirit that they were in that put it forth." This is the way: not just to read or understand theoretically, but to "know" spiritual themes. The very spirit that created them is in us and can know them. What kindergartners say as a taunt applies as a positive in the highest sphere: "It takes One to know One."

Higher Order Distractions

In the midst of the meditation, a subtle sense of guidance can arise. It is as if our thoughts are guided, aided, by an unseen and loving power. It may be simply that whatever it is within us that recognizes a distraction comes to the fore sooner and more surely redirects us to the chosen theme. We can also get to the point of feeling a guidance or guiding that is both not us, and yet within us. It points the individual meditant who feels it toward a more fruitful area of the theme for him or her to focus on at this moment.

At the same time, this guidance can itself become a distraction, like all special conditions that arise during meditation, including bliss, serenity, experiences of bodily energy, and perceptions of the inner life of others. All these, unless they are the chosen theme of meditation, are simultaneously attainments and distractions. They may represent the good, valid fruit of immersing ourselves in the theme, but they also prevent our deeper immersion if we pause to enjoy them or become fascinated with them. Beginning meditants are often so happy to see a valid result of their efforts that they have great difficulty in renouncing such results for continued work with the theme.

There is nothing really wrong with enjoying such results, either. It's just that if you do, you stop there. In the ideal case, you don't pause to notice the fruits of meditation until the meditation is over. There will be all the more to marvel over, the more you have renounced marvels along the way.

Rilke, in the first of the *Duino Elegies,* says that he wants to listen for inspiration the way the great listeners of the Middle Ages listened for God's speech. He says that they listened so well, so intently, that the "answering call" from heaven lifted them bodily off the floor. So here is a monk, say, or simply a person lost in prayer, and they are hovering, in a kneeling position, in mid-air. "And they," writes Rilke, "the impossible ones, didn't notice."

That would be a strong attention: that you would be so involved in the theme of concentration that you did not notice your body was hovering in the air. For most of us, this would be impossible. Attention, weakening from its chosen theme, would collapse back onto the physical body as it so often does, and we would notice our hovering, and crash to the floor. "I have done well," writes Emerson, "I see that I have done well, and lo, it is the beginning of ill."

"Uses" of the World of Light

Through meditation, much insight and opening may come about at the edges of the theme. We are tempted to turn aside and make a note, or to revel in the new understanding that has come. But instead we renounce all of this for the time being and keep returning, returning, returning to the chosen focus. At other times, however, this tendency of meditation to bring us into a wider awareness can be adapted to problem-solving, as long as we are clear about the total game plan.

There is a story that a group of businessmen came to the Baal Shem Tov to ask for his help in a delicate negotiation they were about to have in a distant city. The Baal Shem asked for a Torah to be brought to him, and he opened it, reading deeply. After some minutes, he looked up and told them what they should do in their negotiations and just how the affair would turn out if they followed his advice.

They thanked him and went on their way. Sure enough, it all took place just as he had said. One of the men passed through the village of the Baal Shem on his return journey. He stopped in to thank the rabbi. He also had a question for him. "When you helped us and asked for a Torah to read in," he asked, "were you looking for a passage relevant to our difficulties, to apply the message of Scripture?"

"Oh, no," said the master. "I read the holy text for its own sake, opening it at random. Immersion in its life-giving words brings me into the world of light. There, everything is clear. So, of course, I see what is to be done in your particular troubles."

The moral of this tale is not exactly that scripture can be used. That would be a disastrous shift of emphasis. Please do not come away from this anecdote with the notion, "Now I see how to turn these silly old books to good account!" In a sense, the Baal Shem was indeed using Torah for earthly, everyday purposes. But this could work only because of his capacity to forget precisely the business application and to read the holy text for its own sake.

By all means, think of some practical or personal issue in your life on the way into the meditation. And think of it again, by all means, at the end of the meditation. You may well see more clearly into the subject because of the elevation, the intensification of consciousness that meditation gave you. But during the meditation itself, the theme alone lives, the "problem" you frame it with need not appear to you at all, and if it does, it is just another distraction, and worthy of not the slightest lingering notice. The world of light is not for our selfish use, but it is absolutely available to our needs when these are integrated into the whole. Just this balance is what the Baal Shem achieved through his immersion in the law.

GOOD MEDITATION AND GOOD ENOUGH MEDITATION

One measure of success in meditation is the feeling of having grown more intimate with the theme. We "catch" it higher upstream, nearer its sources. The theme becomes alive, uncontrollable, exciting, while remaining all the more that theme with which we started. This is the most basic, funda-mental, measure of the meditation: the theme means more.

There are other consequences of a happy meditation. One is the feeling of release. We excarnate a bit. That is, we come loose from all our "bodies"—the physical body, the emotional body, the memory body, the body of habits and restraints, the body of our language, the body of our prejudices. Ram Dass quoted a friend as saying, "Death is like taking off a tight shoe." In group meditation, we can feel this kind of relief and expansive freedom. We loosen the tight shoe of our daily world and self.

Another such feature is the feeling of friendliness. People in the group toward whom you feel some closeness, some antipathy, suddenly become understandable, approachable, lovable. This, too, comes from our release from the world of things, at the subtle epistemological level of participation in the theme, which is no longer an object to understand separate from ourselves.

One day a member of the group looked up from the piece of gravel he was using in a group exercise of meditative perception. It was just a piece of gray, unromantic gravel, of the kind we were all focusing on—nothing sexy or sentimental like quartz or jade. But from his intense involvement in the gravel he looked up with a smile and declared, "I want to announce that I feel this unaccountable friendliness toward everyone here." He had come outside himself and into the gravel—but into the gravel as a divine meaning, which immediately delivers us into a different stance toward the people around us. A peaceful stance, you could say.

All these and many other markers may arise to persuade you of the value of your meditation. But it is good enough if you do meditate, and at least recognize when you are or are not distracted; at least recognize when you do and do not have fresh thoughts. Even a "bad" meditation, in which you were actively willing to experiment but felt you got no "result," is certainly good enough and will have its benefits. We turn our will over to the will of the universe as it operates behind the theme, regardless of results. We say, "Thy will be done." Thomas Kelly put it this way: "*If the wills have been offered together in the silent work of worship*, worshipers may still go home content and nourished and say, 'It was a good meeting.'"

DEMONS AWAKEN

It can also happen that the intense focus of meditation increases both our all-too-familiar fixed forms of thought and feeling, and also some apparently unfamiliar and alarming forms. This may surprise and distress us at times. Here we are taking the time to meditate, supposedly a progressive and salutary process, and it's making everything worse. We have terrible, ugly thoughts and unacceptable feelings.

This problem has two roots. On the one hand, we may simply be noticing more forms that were already present. The heightened alertness of meditative focus brings into view everything within the soul. Desires, angers, jealousies, doubts, and so on, all seem to grow because we only now have the objectivity, the clarity, the wakefulness, to detect them. We find that boredom, worries, fears, assail us as never before.

It is as if there were a broken pot that had been glued back together imperfectly. As a light rises behind the pot its cracks, already evident, become far more evident. The very light that will bring joy and make it possible to use the pot or repair or replace it is the light by which, initially, we see its flaws as never before. This process is known as an encounter with the "guardian of the threshold."

It is enough that we see the guardian, the cracks, the flaws. That is the encounter. We don't need to linger with it. There is a danger of being hypnotized by our failings, seduced away from pursuit of the meditation by the guardian's painfully accurate slurs against our character. If we absolutely cannot relinquish our fascination with our own flaws, we are not ready to meditate just now.

On the other hand, and more mysteriously still, our efforts seem to attract unfamiliar and unwholesome inner elements. We can understand it in this way: the extra energy of attention produced by meditation needs somewhere to go, and if we are not utterly immersed in the subject of the meditation, this extra energy will inflate all kinds of forms, both old and new. It energizes them. Then, too, whatever in us really doesn't want our well-being, and desires our ill, seems to redouble its efforts to divert us just as we make our own efforts to leave the realm of fixed forms.

How to Deal with the Demons

No matter how dreadful the inner feelings and visions may be that come to besiege a meditation, they have no greater dignity than the silliest distraction. C. S. Lewis said that one of the devil's greatest weapons is to make us think that he doesn't exist. Perhaps this is so. But another of his greatest weapons must be to make us think that he does exist. Rather than be blown off course by the miserable thought or the devilish apparition, we can, as with any distraction, simply let go and find our way back to the theme. One way of formulating the goal of meditation, as we have said, is just this: the theme grows, while all else fades.

There is only one threshold. We cannot cross the threshold without encountering the possibility of descent. In this sense, it is good news that we are attacked by inner demons. It means we are approaching or crossing the threshold of valid spiritual experience. But that is where the benefit ends. No further need to engage with them! That would be the realm of psychotherapy. In meditation, we do not suppress or repress them, but we do turn from them toward the theme. This turning diminishes them. If the demons do not eventually disappear, psychotherapy may be a necessary accompaniment or preliminary to further inner work.

In the iconography of the early Christian era up through the dawn of the Middle Ages, St. Michael and St. George were never portrayed as looking directly at the dragon they were slaying. Instead, they looked up to Heaven, or out to the viewer, or forward to their mission, while their sword or spear killed the dragon effortlessly. This image can serve us in meditation and many other moments in life. It is not by direct attack that the dragon is killed, but by being skillfully ignored.

A certain good will is required for a group to meditate together. This good will becomes the momentum that carries the group further and further into a capacity to do group work. If the will is not there to open, in all humility, to the theme of the meditation, if the will is not there to let the theme itself restructure us in our core, then the group meetings become false. People start to spout fake-holy, formulaic truisms instead of speaking truth. They speak as they think meditants should speak. They speak what they would like to experience, what sounds spiritual, what they have read. The actual, active peace between Heaven and Earth is closed off, and the group starts to lose direction. Soon interpersonal problems start to come up between group members, and things can go from glorious to good to fair to bad. And then worse. The spirit of falsity and division is having its way with the group.

On the bright side, we can always recover. The cure, of course, is for anyone who notices the ills of the group themselves to manifest the good will to forgive themselves and the others and dive into the theme with renewed attention. One person's wholehearted re-dedication of devotion will lead to a similar re-dedication on the part of others. This may be preceded by someone in the group saying that they feel the group has gone awry, but we cannot solve group problems by discussion and intellection. Criticisms of the group tend all too easily to contribute to the condition to which they refer. The cure for bad meditation is more and better meditation, nothing else.

What is Quicker than Light?

In his handmade fairy tale, "The Green Snake and the White Lily," Goethe asks, "What is livelier than light?" The answer turns out to be *conversation*.

The German word he uses, *erquicklicher,* means "lively," "nourishing," but we hear in it also the "quick" of both "the quick and the dead," and "quick service." It refers to instantaneous nourishment. A good conversation can miraculously translate you out of suffering selfhood and into the clarity of shared life with others. Any conversation can become, suddenly, a shared meal, nourishing beyond expectation.

What is the magic ingredient in this meal? I am struck by how often my patients, whether describing a fight or an intimate moment, apologize for the paltry, unimpressive content of the interaction in question. It was just about letting the cat in. It was just a touch of the hand. It was just the way he put the plate on the counter. It was just a fight about which lightbulb to buy. But the apparent content of a moment of healing or a moment of hurting is never the real issue. What matters is the quality of attention, the unspoken, unspeakable motivation behind the words, which can make any slightest interaction a blessing or a curse.

Quick wit in conversation will sometimes suggest more than it delivers, but this suggestion is everything. We feel the approach of a realm of possibility, a spirit of humor and connection that far exceeds the joke or pun manifested. Famously, when we try to repeat something of a witty conversation it never seems as good as it did originally. "You had to be there," we say.

When, in meditation, we have the presence of mind needed for a sparkling volley of wit, then the background spirits of the theme come close and the experience is obviously one of conversation.

ANCHOR

One prepares the way for many. It helps the group if one person prepares the ground for the meditation by having a meditative practice outside the group practice. The more members of the group who do this, the better it is for the group as a whole; but let there be at least one. It is not important that that person meditate on the coming group theme, which may in any case remain undecided until the last moment. What matters is that those who meditate beforehand have attempted to intensify their exact wonder at the knowability of the world.

There is a speculation by Kafka in which he imagines the great globe turning in space. Some people are awake, some asleep. But even if everyone were asleep at once, he says, over the whole Earth, at least one person would need to be awake. Each of us feels the call at moments to be that one who stays awake for the sake of the planet, or at least for our meditation group.

REPORTS

Reporting is the last phase of meditation. After we open our eyes, we bring news to the others, news of the theme, which stimulates their continuing entry into it, and that is the whole point. The listening to the report is the reason for the report, or rather, listening through the report to the theme beyond it. Something of what the reporting meditant experienced of the theme is present, hovering behind what the meditant says. This hovering presence leads the attentive listener into further depths of the theme. In a sense, then, the report only obscures the theme if we focus on it too much. It is best seen as another form of the theme being stated by the reporter. Since the reporter is bothering to put into words an experience of the theme, the need of the listeners to have words and images go on in the mind is ensured, and the listeners are potentially liberated during the report to have a completely nonverbal, non-imagistic experience of the theme, perhaps beyond anything the reporter describes or experiences.

The fifteenth-century Swiss Saint Bruder Klaus did not eat for twenty years. He was nourished from another source. He did not boast about it, never wrote about it, did not have a "method," and was not as interested in his "miraculous fasting" as others were. On one occasion he confided to a visitor that, when he watched others take communion in the little chapel by his cell, he was so nourished by their reception of the divine substance that he needed no other nourishment himself. His meat and drink was to see others receive the holy bread and wine.

Something like this happens to each of us when we listen to meditation reports. Without trying to, without wishing it, we receive a redoubled measure of access to the theme through noticing its presence in and behind our friends.

There is no "should" in meditation. The whole procedure takes place under the sign of freedom. Therefore, no one "should" report on their experience. No one need feel an obligation or expectation to report. Still, we can report, and at times it's good if we do.

Reports are not autobiography. They are not meant to be complete accounts of one's experience during the meditation, with all its ups and downs. As listeners, we want only the cream, the freshest experience of the theme itself. If your heart chakra got all warm and glowing, if you remembered a touching moment from childhood, a story you once heard, a beautiful poem or piece of scripture that seems related—well, that may have been your experience during the meditation, but it was not your current experience of the theme itself, and it is better left out of your report. There is always a kind of abdication of one's responsibility to the theme when reporting falls into items culled from memory.

The ideal reporting, then, has nothing in it of the travelogue. It is not a psychological or emotional story of the meditation one has just had. Rather, it is a direct speaking from the theme's presence either as the theme presented itself during the period of closed-eyes meditation or as it presents itself now, in the moment of reporting. There are many accounts of speech like this, for example from the Chasidic master of the nineteenth century, Rabbi Dov Baer of Mezeritch. He once said, "When I am discoursing on a subject of Torah [that is, revelation] I neither hear nor feel the words I am speaking. They issue from my mouth without my knowledge or help. As soon as I hear myself talking, I stop."

SILENCE

Though our meditations typically have a theme, the theme always reverts to silence.

First, the theme emerges from silence. It is our listening silence, in advance, that invites the theme to reveal itself within us. Emerson: "I like the silent church, before the service begins, better than any preaching." It is by no means easy, in the heart and mind, to construct, so to speak, the inner temple quiet enough to receive the theme's Word in its ever-newness.

Second, the theme is nourished out of silence—the pregnant void between our thoughts, just before the next understanding comes, or just before we descend into distraction.

Third, when a meditation comes to its end, we can find that the silence we enjoy afterward, sometimes in a hushed and holy awe, resonates with the power of our immersion. At times, we feel we want this post-meditation silence to go on and on. Any words that disturb it or call it to an end feel like a kind of blasphemy.

Finally, we come to sense that the source of all possible meditation and prayer and creativity is itself silence—a silence that both listens and speaks, so a very active silence, but silence nonetheless. We could call it the Open, or the Light, or even the Word.

SILENCE

The one who's more inwardly silent
Touches on the roots of speech.
One day, every syllable of his will be victory
Over what, in the silence, isn't silent,
Over the mocking of evil.
The Word was shown to him for this:
To dissolve himself tracelessly.

—RAINER MARIA RILKE

PART TWO
PRACTICE OF GROUP MEDITATION

Preparation

Many practices can be undertaken to prepare for group meetings. As we suggested earlier, these can anchor and deepen the group work. They include individual meditation, exercises to develop concentration generally, and in particular exercises undertaken to awaken the life of feeling. Some of them will be discussed here. What matters most is that these practices, like group meditation itself, stay light and improvisatory: stay real.

STIGA

To begin the process of the transformation of feeling, we can engage with feelings we all know, but that are already a bit less about ourselves, a bit more about the world around us. They are subjective, certainly, and have the lively warmth of emotional experience, but the balance within them tips more toward informing us than indulging us. Normally, we just stumble into these feelings, but it is possible to practice them and so make them into directable, intentional forces that increase our capacity for intimacy, actually of all kinds.

Here are five such feelings, complete with suggestions for how to intensify their benefits. *STIGA* is an acronym for these five: Surprised, Touched, Inspired, Grateful, and Amused.

Surprised

Let yourself notice what surprised you today. It need not be something important, and it need not be positive. As you recall it, see if you can be surprised again by it.

You might object that it cannot be surprising now, since it is a memory, after all, and you already know about the thing. For example, you were surprised that the rain lasted all day. How can you be surprised at that now, seeing that you already know it?

This intentionality is a key feature of the exercise. We make ourselves like those Method actors who generate a real feeling to portray it on stage. They are not only acting sad; they also make themselves truly sad. It may take some doing to generate the feeling of surprise again. You may have to imagine looking at the rain and at the clock, or saying to someone, "Wow, it's still raining!"—or invent other ways to stimulate an actual sense of surprise at the rain.

It can be helpful to write down what it was that surprised you. This has a way of focusing you on the task, and also of confirming for you that this day has contained a surprise. With repeated practice, your days become more surprising altogether. Surprises may be positive, or negative, or just neutral. The emotion in question is not about something being agreeable, or relevant to oneself at all, just surprising or contrary to expectations.

Touched

What touched you today? What moved you, in other words? What did you find poignant? These are all more or less synonyms for the feeling being sought now. Where surprise could be neutral or negative, being touched always involves a measure of positivity. Often, however, it is positive only to the point of being bittersweet.

For example, I was touched today by a child patient who struggles with his obesity. There is sorrow and something very wrong with the picture at hand, but there is something beautiful in his attempt to master both his poor habits and his own terrible self-criticism. His struggle moved me.

Again, we try to write down the experience in a word or two—it need not be a full account at all—and while writing to feel the feeling once again. Sometimes the words and images and thoughts required to generate the feeling in retrospect take a few minutes, which may be much longer than the original experience. It is worth the trouble. Your entire world becomes more poignant, more touching, more moving, as a result of repeating this exercise over some weeks.

Inspired

What inspired you today? What filled you with awe or wonder?

Once I suggested to a client that he find something to think about on his way into sleep that would fill him with wonder, like a great achievement in science or sports. He said, "But that would humiliate me, of course." Say what? It turned out he meant that since he didn't feel he had achieved anything much in life, thinking about anyone else's achievements would necessarily lead to humiliation as he compared this other person with himself. But comparing the other person with himself, however automatic or understandable, had nothing to do with the task at hand. It was a self-referential detour from the practice of awe, a souring of the original project.

In this exercise, we try to stay with the feeling of awe or wonder for a bit, and not let it take any automatic emotional nosedive—into humiliation or anything else. Inspired is unambiguously positive, unlike both Surprised and Touched. Some people say the sunset "inspired me to..." and then follows a project of their own. However, what nourishes us here, the turning outward of emotional energy so that it becomes feeling, does not have to do with what we are inspired to do, but with what inspires us. The emphasis remains outward, not pointing to us or our future projects. In good time, of course, we want to be inspired to do. But for now, for this practice, allow yourself to linger in the moment of awe.

Grateful

When were you thankful, grateful, today? What made you feel that feeling of gratitude? What was it about the action or event that inspired this feeling? Allow yourself, perhaps as you write down the experience, to feel thankful once again.

Here as in all the **STIGA** exercises, please do not excuse yourself from the practice on the grounds that you were not grateful for anything today, or not surprised by anything today, or not touched, etc. If, in reviewing the day, there is really nothing for which you felt grateful, then feel grateful for some aspect of the day now, as you do the exercise. Just decide on something and generate the feeling, even though you did not feel it at the time. For example, you got on a bus and traveled across town today. In real life, during the bus ride your mind was just occupied with the friend you were going to see. Now, in retrospect, you can instead generate gratitude for the driver's efforts in shepherding you and the other passengers to their destinations. Think about the driver's training, perhaps, or recall some helpful gesture he made toward a passenger, and see if you can conjure the experience of gratitude.

Amused

What was funny today? What amused you? What made you laugh or at least smile?

The natural, unforced, unself-conscious smile is one of the best things we can provide for ourselves or another person. Sometimes it is very difficult to bring a true smile about. We have to put ourselves in harm's way, as it were. We have to expose ourselves to the danger of a humorous person or situation. I knew a woman who always called a particular friend when she was sad not because he would give her good advice—he never did—but only because he could make her laugh, talking about things that had nothing to do with her problems. The procedure was artificial in that she intentionally called him. Once the conversation got rolling, a paradox reliably unfurled: humor both spontaneous and intentional.

In this exercise, maybe the hardest of the lot, we try once again to be tickled, amused, laughing, over something that happened or was said earlier in the day. You will see, as soon as you try to do this, that it requires an extra measure of good will, a kind of willed innocence. In the classic *Black Elk Speaks,* the old medicine man recounts how in his youth, on the reservation, he and his friends could laugh at the same silly joke over and over throughout the winter, and find it just as funny in the spring. He remarked that the white people had lost the power of renewable humor. It can be recovered.

The unforced but intentional smile also serves as a basis for any meditation, even one on a serious or sad theme. The inner leavening that comes from your smile (a slight, Mona Lisa smile, as Thich Nhat Hanh recommends) leads to new insight, openness, willingness, readiness.

These **STIGA** exercises are a method for reviving the feeling life in several ways. Not only is adult emotional life normally too self-directed and non-cognitive; it is also passive, negatively tinged, and relatively dead or dormant. Practices that turn emotional energy outward, toward the world, also tend to enliven it and render it more positively tinged. Your world becomes less tame, more vibrant. And this greater vibrancy does not take place among familiar feelings or emotions alone. Rather, as the eye can sense an infinity of shapes and colors, the heart can feel an infinite variety of qualities within the world, other people, and all manner of processes that surround us—from the cries of birds at dawn to the wheeling of stars at night to the jostle of crowds on the subway at rush hour.

STRUCTURE OF GROUP MEDITATION PRACTICE

For group meditation, it is necessary, and it is sufficient, for two or more people to reach together toward the source of a meaning they have agreed to explore. There is no method or structure that can guarantee the quality of this activity. Still, to make collaboration more likely, a certain structure may be helpful. This section puts into an overview the format of group practice out of which this book is written. Groups may find completely different formats that work for them. It is best to experiment somewhat even with a beloved format to keep from imagining that the format by itself guarantees, or is, meditation.

The practice suggested here begins with the selection of a group theme. Then the theme is discussed within the group. After some time of discussion, the decision is made to be silent, close one's eyes perhaps, and focus individually on the chosen theme. When the meditation is over, group members have a chance to share reports on their experience of the theme. A schema of the process might look like this:

1.   A theme is chosen.
2.   Discussion of the theme.
3.   Closed-eye meditation.
   - Do something first
   - Ponder the theme
   - Deal with distractions
   - Reduction
   - Slowing down
   - The theme takes over
   - Do something last
4.   Reports of the meditation.
   - No need to report
   - No cross-talk
   - Only your experience
   - What about live experience?
   - Do not persuade
5.   Restatement of the theme.

A Theme Is Chosen

In an earlier section, we saw that sample themes can come from any tradition and need not even be "spiritual" in an overt sense. Fundamentally, we cannot wander from the spirit, since we perceive and think by the same spirit that made the world and all that is in it. As Carl Jung wrote above his library door, "Invoked or not invoked, God is present."

How then, to choose a theme from the infinite variety of texts and situations and events and objects that may have a high source? That is the question that looms as soon as we leave the safety of a traditional setting or the authority of a "master."

In practice, however, it is a bit of a pseudo-problem. A group that has practiced together and learned together can often meditate satisfyingly with a completely new, strange meditative theme of a kind they never worked with before. They may also feel a real benefit from the slow build-up through related themes that they have dwelt on together over months or years. What matters, above all, is the intensity of the shared practice, the willingness to open within concentration, rather than the exact theme. Every worthwhile theme, taken far enough, will shock us, and may contain elements that seem unacceptable as we immerse ourselves in it. Every theme, too, offers ample opportunity to learn about distractions and how to deal with them.

I have worked with a small group, for example, on the koans or "public cases" in a collection called *The Blue Cliff Record.* These are demanding meditations that insist on our leaving our normal mind right from the start. They can be thought about, pondered over, but not exactly "figured out." They are impervious to our urge to understand in a dualistic way, but they can be understood nonetheless, if we have the good will and persistence. In order to choose them, however, the group had to be willing to dive into the terms and style of medieval Chinese Buddhism. The book with its hundred koans gave us a kind of structure for a time, but we did not rigidly plow through the koans in sequence. Rather, we metaphorically rapped on each one to see if it would open to us; those that "gave" we opened a bit further through meditation. But we did this sometimes quite out of sequence, and we allowed ourselves to intersperse the process with other meditations from other traditions, always returning to the *Blue Cliff* for its nourishing frustrations. This took some years.

In another group, we have worked in chunks of meditations related to an overarching thematic. For example, we spent some months following the major festivals of the Christian year, seeking renewed life within traditional vocabulary and stories that had become all too familiar, all too predictable, and in fact meaningless for most of us. Through our joint work, passages we had heard all our lives sprang to new relevance and vibrancy, revealing facets we would never have dreamed existed.

We have also at times worked through books together (notably Georg. Kühlewind's *The Light of the "I"* and Massimo Scaligero's *The Light),* taking themes from them not as theory or theology but as meditations—that is, direct runways into the heavens. The runway is not the sky, but it leads to the sky if you use it to fly. To use a book in this way means that either the group leader, if there is one, or the group as a whole, selects specific passages or phrases that seem promising. The process of selection itself, if it is a group undertaking, contributes to the strength of focus required to let the theme focused on dissolve in its initial meanings and permit its wider range of senses to shine through.

At times I have worked with groups on sequences of images, such as those that emerge from healing stories, parables, or religious paintings. What keeps these from being "graven images" in any negative sense is that we do not mistake the runway for the sky.

DISCUSSION OF THE THEME

It wakes us up and challenges us when we thrash through the theme together, out loud, before we close our eyes and meditate on it. We pick a passage of a text, or a specific sentence, or an image or object, and then we talk through its meanings. The discussion may reveal sharp differences of interpretation among us. Sometimes the discussion takes off and has wings; sometimes it sits there like a dead thing. As long as we stay open to the theme, the discussion ends up uniting us in spite of ourselves.

By inviting everyone's participation, preliminary discussion brings all of us into closer contact with the theme. Still, no one is forced to speak and there should be no sense of taking turns. You speak if you have something to say—often, this means having something to ask.

Entry into this discussion presents us with something like the difference between being a passenger and being the driver in a car. You take more responsibility as the driver. If you just listen to a group leader talk about the theme, you remain relatively passive. If everyone contributes, everyone becomes an active leader of the group. Group discussion thus belongs to the egalitarian, democratic tendency of group meditation. Leadership does not really reside in any particular human being: our true guide is the reality of the theme.

It is during this initial, discussion phase that we might mention any relevant memories—what the theme reminds us of, what it is like. We may bring out quotations, anecdotes, analogies. We talk back and forth with each other, maybe interrupting each other, in the manner of a lively family dinner-table debate.

Later, in closed-eyes meditation itself, as well as in the subsequent reporting, we try precisely not to rely on content from out of memory. We think and feel our way into the theme as if for the first time. Memories of the prior discussion may come back to us, but they are not essential. The discussion did its work of orientation and we need not consciously refer to it in our own minds when we later meditate.

Discussion of the theme does not mean arriving at conclusions about the theme. We may start with a passage from the Upanishads or the Bible or the Sutras, and some members of the group may have something helpful to say about the passage that places it in historical or theological context. There may be deep and compelling readings of the theme that someone can cite to educate us. None of this means we have had an experiential encounter with the theme.

When Hamlet overhears Claudius, his evil uncle, at prayer, he resolves not to kill him yet; he wants to kill him when he is spiritually vulnerable, rather than when reconciled to God. But Hamlet doesn't know what we, the audience, know: that Claudius is having a hard time at prayer. And he complains of his own worried, guilt-ridden mind, "My words fly up, my thoughts remain below. Words without thoughts never to Heaven go." The discussion of the theme aligns our words with our thoughts, so that our subsequent meditation can ascend.

Sometimes, at the very first instant the theme is seriously being discussed and the group focus is just beginning to find the theme, a sense of the theme as a background to the group that day is already present, or feels present to some among us. It is as if the theme announces its presence behind, above, or in contradiction to what we are saying about it. "I feel the same truth how often in my trivial conversation with my neighbors," writes Emerson, "that somewhat higher in each of us overlooks this by-play, and Jove nods to Jove from behind each of us."

In an experienced group, the whole "prior" discussion of the theme may in fact already constitute meditation on the theme, with no break in the proceedings. This is the ideal case. Then there is a sense that the vast range of implication within the theme is present and active in the room even though we seem to be only talking, only jawing, only quoting things and repeating other people's experiences. The words of the participants in discussion need not be correct and certainly need not be brilliant for this to occur. But we notice that even broken thoughts, incorrect words, mistaken interpretations, somehow anchor a continuing operation of the theme within us and among us. When we feel this is happening, the experience is both striking and natural. It can hardly be mentioned or referred to for fear of losing it. If made too much of, it will distract us from the theme itself.

Stir the liquid quickly into the dry ingredients, taking only fifteen to twenty seconds in which to do it. Make no attempt to stir or beat out any lumps. Ignore them. Unnecessary handling of the batter results in tough muffins. (Irma Brombauer, *The Joy of Cooking*, 1943)

It is already an achievement, however, if we begin to quiet our minds through the prior discussion, noticing and relinquishing our many distractions. These include any judgments we make about the theme or about the contributions of the group members, whether positive or negative. The theme matters; our judgments of each other do not matter. The theme matters; our frequent distractions from it do not matter. The theme matters; our despair or lack of interest do not matter. As the theme grows and we as separate selves decrease, discussion can come to an end and we can close our eyes to meditate.

A temptation exists, for some participants, to hold on to their best, brightest understanding of the theme and not share it during discussion. It is like a treasure they do not want to lose, but plan to unfurl in the privacy of their own minds during the later meditation proper. Big mistake. A high theme, like the Flower Sermon of the Buddha— in which he simply raises a flower and a single disciple, Kashyapa, understands him—has no limit to its possible range of meanings. We can go right ahead and share our cherished, special understanding. More will come! It is a gift to the group to release to them your very best thoughts, as well as your sharpest, most debilitating doubts. All of these will promote the honesty of the group, on which virtue any further deepening depends.

In a way, our conversation has the aim of exhausting the verbal and imagistic mind. This means that later, when our eyes are closed and we dive into the theme individually, we can more readily let go of our tight hold on habits.

Sometimes the best outcome of prior discussion is simply a sense of the futility of discussion. We sense, "This is not the way to get to the heart of the theme." We sense that we need to approach the life of the theme more directly, more intimately, than words can permit just now. As someone once said, tired of an over-lengthy discussion, "Shall we *do* something?"

CLOSED-EYES MEDITATION

We close our eyes when meditating a verbal or symbolic theme so as not to be distracted by the visual field. There is no danger that we will make it too easy for ourselves. We still have plenty of distractions left. We intentionally set all these aside and engage directly with the chosen theme of meditation. Closing the eyes is a merciful step to begin the process. If closing them all the way brings sleep too automatically, we can half-close them.

While there is no posture that will guarantee entry into a meditative practice, some form of sitting with closed eyes and upright spine is probably the best starting point. Relaxation practices, such as progressive tightening and then release of all the parts of the body, are helpful precisely to the degree that they allow us to forget our body and dive into the meditation. Just as the eyes are not busy seeing, the other senses should not be busy with their work unless we are doing a perceptual meditation specifically working to school and transform the senses. We are seeking:

That serene and blessed mood,
In which the affections gently lead us on,—
Until, the breath of this corporeal frame
And even the motion of our human blood
Almost suspended, we are laid asleep
In body, and become a living soul:
While with an eye made quiet by the power
Of harmony, and the deep power of joy,
We see into the life of things.

WORDSWORTH, "Tintern Abbey"

Do Something First

It is good to enter the theme indirectly by doing a little something after the eyes are closed, perhaps something that lasts a half-a-minute or a minute.

This could be to sing a song inwardly, or dance a jig in your imagination. It could be silently to recite a verse or a prayer with quiet intensity. It could be to stamp your foot mentally, or tell yourself a joke. It could be to go around the room in your mind's eye and thank the other meditants for the silent aid of their presence.

One particularly helpful preliminary gesture of this kind is to think a thought that brings you to the edge of normal consciousness. There are many such "limit" thoughts, and they have the salutary effect of returning you to a point of innocence. For example, you might dare to repeat Heidegger's challenging question: Why is there something, when there could so easily be nothing? Or you might notice that thinking itself, evidence, the capacity to reason, to understand—all this is a gift. We may sharpen our cognitive abilities, but we cannot invent them from scratch. Like the world as a whole, they are just there, as gifts.

Or you might keep yourself teetering on the threshold of the activity of meditation itself, asking yourself: Will I really do this thing? Is it time to begin it? Should I delay a moment longer or launch into it right now? This kind of intentional dithering gathers your energy, heats up your readiness, and fosters your commitment to make this very meditation, this very day, count for something.

Ponder the Theme

Pondering or musing over the theme leads imperceptibly to meditation, as we noted for the preliminary discussion. For at any moment consciousness can rise knowingly into the non-verbal, non-imagistic source-stream from which it is continuously fed. There is therefore a certain artificiality about all talk of stages and methods in meditation. Certainly from this point on, the point of pondering, there need be no further conscious decision to demarcate stages within the process while your are meditating. From this point on, the theme alone matters, and we do not care if there are words or images or if we are doing it right or wrong. We do not worry about distractions, even though we may deal with them. We try not to worry about our neighbor meditants. If we delve deeply into the theme for ourselves, it will also be the best help for them. Afterward, in reviewing the course of meditation, it may matter to us to note when we entered a different level of understanding, or what the trajectory of our meditation was. But for now we make the theme alone important, not the bumpy ride by which we enter it.

To ponder or muse over the theme we bring to mind everything we have already thought, heard or read about it that seems relevant to us just now. We push our previous thoughts a bit further, we let them query their way into us a bit more deeply, we open to their reality a bit more entirely. It may help inwardly to declare the theme, so that we take full responsibility for it. It is not something we are overhearing, but something we ourselves are asserting. We try to find its best meaning, always willing for as-yet-unheard-of aspects to surprise us from as-yet-unsuspected angles. It will not help simply to repeat the words of the theme, if it is a verbal theme, over and over again. They will tend to mean less that way. Meditating them means having them mean far more.

Here, as in the prior discussion phase, it is salutary to object to the theme in every way so as later to affirm it the more intimately. For example, you work with the theme "With God, all things are possible." You might bring to mind that God is supposed to be omnipresent, so we are always with God, yet not all things seem possible—either to you right now, or to others in their hours of need and even torment. It is patently obvious that with or without God (whatever that means) not all things are possible to everyone and everywhere—maybe especially not when it most matters, when "God" or "things" are most needed. So the sentence is nonsense.

This apparently negativistic sequence of reflections turns to good account when we use it to sharpen our sense of what is meant in the sentence by "with" and by "God" and by "things" and by "possible." You don't need to apologize for or justify the theme. You want its full earthly absurdity to come glaringly into the light of attention. By allowing this, and then keeping the mind wondering and open, you also invite the theme in its power gradually to convince you, if that is in the way of things.

And we do want and need to be convinced. "Convince," by its Latin roots, means "to conquer collaboratively." We want the theme to swamp or vanquish all our own objections to it. For this convincement to be adequate, our skepticism needs to be great, our objections searching and cold-eyed. If we then manage to overcome them satisfyingly, the victory is much greater than if it were all easy affirmation from the get-go. This was also the method of Thomas Aquinas. He would present the case against a true proposition so cogently that it seemed he had destroyed the proposition utterly. Then his rebuttal, his arguments for the proposition, would establish it with a more blazing sense of evidence.

To ponder, take a sentence like the question asked of Adam in Genesis 2:8: "Where are you?" We first situate it perhaps in its context in the biblical story of the Fall. We notice that the story centers around considerations of place: the Garden, the tree in its center, the coming expulsion. It is very much about location. But after eating, Adam and Eve hide themselves. They are nowhere to be found. God asks, "Where are you?" We cannot imagine that he does not know this in a geographical sense. They could hardly get far, on foot, from that all-seeing eye. We can imagine rather that Adam hid inside himself, as we all can do in our guilt, even if the question of "where" included physical space. Either way, Adam could not escape from God, any more than Jonah could escape on shipboard or in the belly of a whale later in the story. The ground of being knows very well where Adam is, where you are, where I am, so the question is not a question to get information, but perhaps a question to make the one of whom it is asked undertake an inner search. This could include varying the question from Where are you? to Who are you? and How (in what way) are you? and even Why are you? We can refresh the question by allowing it to be asked of us directly, right now, in the act of pondering it. We can ask it ourselves either of divinities, humans, or other aspects of the world, and notice our essential nature as related beings, creatures of relationship. We may notice that there is no verbal formula that could answer the question, but the question is rather answered by our whole selves, our very being, our embodied self-declaration.

There is no limit to the depth and the variety of possible ponderings. Let your thinking about the theme become absorbing, to the point that it becomes a real event in your life, a consideration that changes you.

DEAL WITH DISTRACTIONS

We deal with every distraction, of whatever kind, whether from Heaven or Hell, by lightly returning to the theme as soon as a distraction is noticed. There are at least three methods to consider.

The first applies in the case of extended distractions in the form of "trains of thought" that have taken you far from the theme. In such cases, you can intentionally travel back along the path you wandered, until you return to the theme or to the original distraction from it. For example, you are meditating "God is light" and as part of the pondering you reflect that this is not physical light, like the light from a lightbulb. Then you notice that the natural light in the room is adequate, there is no reason for the ceiling light to be on, especially with everyone's eyes closed in meditation. Then you reflect that a new member of the group was asking why we do close our eyes in meditation. Then you recall that this new member was invited into the group by your friend Paul. At this point, you notice that you are not with "God is light," and you resolve to return to the theme by the same path you took to leave it. So you realize you were just thinking of Paul, before that of the new member who asked about closed eyes, before that about the ceiling light, before that about the distinction between various kinds of light—and now you can continue the meditation just where you left off. This whole procedure takes very little time, and gives a special sense of strength. You realize that instead of being entirely asleep or dreaming during the distraction, you were there all along.

Another technique is to incorporate the distraction into the meditation itself. For example, you meditate the phrase, "This mind is the Buddha." A car starting up noisily outside distracts you. You can imagine the Buddha driving that car, and say to yourself, "This car is the Buddha," and with this humorous reflection return to the theme. If you practice this technique many times, it gives you the palpable sense that your power of return is greater than the power of distraction.

A third approach involves taking the distraction seriously and, so to speak, daring it to matter. You notice, for example, that your mind has wandered to the traffic outside. Well, that isn't the theme. Does the traffic matter? Is that really what you want to spend your time on? Of course it matters very much that we break into the Earth to suck so much petroleum out of it to make these cars and industrial processes operate, with dire environmental consequences. But again, is that really what you want to spend your time on just now? Pause to give the distraction its full dignity, especially if it is a repeat offender against your concentration. Then deliberately, slowly, almost reluctantly, see if you can decide nonetheless to return to the theme and make it new.

REDUCTION

After pondering the theme and letting it intensify by returning to it repeatedly from any distractions, it can happen that every word of the theme means more than it seemed to mean before. On first hearing the theme, or when thinking about it before it became a meditation theme, we may have felt that we already knew what it meant. Our pondering now may have rendered the theme fresh, unfamiliar, surprising, and questionable. As a consequence, every word of the theme can become a revelation.

Take a theme like "Man is a stream whose source is hidden," from Emerson's essay, "The Oversoul." "Man" here certainly means "man and woman," and certainly also includes "child." But what is a human being, after all? Just a primate among others? Is this sentence of Emerson's itself a kind of definition of the human? We realize that we do not quite know what a human is, in essence. Nor do we know what "is" means in the context of the sentence: perhaps that the human "could be" such a stream? And again, in what way is a human being a "stream"? How does Emerson know its source is hidden? Must it remain hidden? Does this have to do with the hiddenness of *lethe* and its lifting through *a-letheia* or truth? How could I find the source? Is it the stream into which Buddha cast his bowl, so that it floated upstream? I am willing to notice the stream of my experience and wonder about its source.

As we do this unpacking, each word of the sentence acquires at times a fractal quality, and summarizes the whole of the thought, the whole of the sentence. *Man* starts to mean precisely the creature whose source is hidden, essentially revealed in the very act of noticing his hiddenness. *Stream* starts to mean just this stream that is the ongoing self-revelation of the human occurrence in the act of meditation. Each word contains the whole, even tiny words like *a* and *whose*. It can happen, though, that one word out of the sentence in particular, just on this particular occasion, calls out to you. The word gives way a bit under the pressure of your attention, or opens to your passionate knocking. The result is that the whole of the sentence, and also the sentence-as-a-whole-as-it-lives-in-each-word, comes to reside in this particular word. You only now have this one word in mind, but it is heavy with the meanings that the pondering has previously brought to mind.

As you focus on the richer significance of this one, ripe word, your further sensing of its range of meaning cannot now proceed by words, since you have given up all but the one word. This one word means so much precisely because you no longer are engaged in word-thinking, but in a kind of alert feeling through this word to its background. Thinking (in words and images) cannot handle the immensity of the theme. Only feeling, the mother of thinking, can sense the whole of the theme and even a greater reach within which the theme lives, behind the single word you have chosen.

At this point of reduction, the intensely meaningful word on which you are focusing has a way of disappearing without your effort. It just isn't in the center of your consciousness any more. It falls away to the degree that the feeling or sensing, the guessing-in-feeling takes over and welcomes further news from the neighborhood of the theme's origins. By this time, the theme has ceased to be abstract or speculative, but has grown visceral, alive, even dangerous. You allow yourself to be changed by a present force that is not of your own making.

Reduction can also happen as an intentional sequence. You think first, "Man is a stream whose source is hidden," then "Man is a stream whose source is," then "Man is a stream whose source," and so on, leaving off one word at a time while keeping the whole meaning intact. Finally you drop "Man" and the whole sentence, as a meaning, lives in you without words. This will go better, and you will be able to "hold" it longer, depending on previous practice with attention.

SLOWING DOWN

At the beginning of our meditations, and for that matter at the beginning of the discussions, we need a lot of material to keep the flow going. It seems there are so many thoughts to think, insights to have, quotations or memories or analogies to bring to bear on the theme. And if these go missing, then thinking comes to an impoverished standstill. There is almost a kind of greed in all this, a need to get another idea about the theme, or even to get the best idea. Behind the greed we may sense a kind of anxiety, a fear that we will be at a loss, or lose ourselves completely, if we don't fill our minds, or the airwaves, with a lot of stuff.

As we continue, though, something surprising can happen. The greed or anxiety subsides. We no longer need to rush in to the conversation, or even to our own next thoughts, with some new perspective, some interesting parallel. Our thoughts slow down. We rest content with what has already been thought, but this is what Aldous Huxley calls "active relaxation." The Tibetans say, "Mix your mind with the sky." In that openness, we do not grasp, but we let what we already know about the theme sink in more deeply, and at the same time we sink into it, and it becomes strangely alive. Now, is it something steady or something changing?

Emily Dickinson might have been provoking us to this quality of inquiry with her poem "The Secret":

Some things that fly there be, —
Birds, hours, the Bumble-bee:
Of these no elegy.

Some things that stay there be, —
Grief, hills, eternity:
Nor this behooveth me.

There are, that resting, rise.
Can I expound the skies?
How still the riddle lies!

THE THEME TAKES OVER

As thinking slows down, it sinks into the guiding feeling, the feeling-for-the-theme, that contains it and directs it. We are still with the theme, but we may have forgotten the words of the theme altogether, or the image of the theme if it started with an image. We are swimming or sculpting in an invisible, non-verbal, non-imagistic medium, and even if images or words are present, they are not the focus or the point of the whole procedure. They are flotsam and jetsam at the edge of awareness.

To reach this state requires an open hand. We do not clutch. So often, in reports of their meditation, meditants will say, "All I could get was...," and there follows often a beautiful insight, but one they could not let go of, once they got it, to allow a next or deeper encounter. The point is not that it is better to have always-new material come in, but simply that it is good to develop the non-grasping mind that remains focused and improvising.

There may have been much effort along the way: effort to find the theme, to make the theme, to search for its reality and its relevance. There may have been much effort to deal with distractions and to return from them many times to the theme itself. But at some point or at several points the theme takes over. I am no longer here, separate from the theme, operating on it or making efforts with it or approaching it or even waiting for it. Rather, the theme becomes myself, or I become the theme, informed by it not from outside myself or even inside myself, but as myself.

It is on the far side of such identity with the theme that the meditation becomes most valuable and also most difficult to describe. For a split second, we become whatever we understand, at any level of cognition. Only later, infinitesimally later, do we stand over against it and "have" it in consciousness. Meditation can be described as a dwelling in that all-too-easily forgotten primal identity with the world that we continually touch on, and continuously lose, in every waking moment. As our work with meditation continues, we find that we can stay awake longer at the point of identity we normally sleep through. It is not exactly that the theme is then in control of us, but rather that both theme and meditant achieve new dignity through this process.

When the theme takes over, it is both something we are doing and something that does us. We are continuing our activity, yet this activity of understanding, thinking, is buoyed up and supported by something else, the very life of the theme. Instead of distractions, we may notice, without losing our involvement, that there are surges and ebbs in the flowing power of attentiveness. No longer striving to stay with the theme, no longer bound by prejudices about its nature, no longer heeding the call of distraction, the meditant is free.

DO SOMETHING LAST

At some point the bell rings, or the time-keeper says to stop, or in some other previously agreed-upon way, the meditation ends. The main consideration in length of time for a meditation is whether or not the majority of people can work with the theme fruitfully during the span in question. Five minutes could be too long; an hour could be too short. Please be honest with yourself and with the group.

Whenever it does end, it is a good practice to "do something" inwardly, just at the end of the meditation, that corresponds to the little "something" you did just at the start. This could be a repetition of the verse or prayer or gesture of thanks you said to yourself privately, or it could be a moment of letting your eyes dwell briefly on an object of the natural world that may strike you with a special resonance because of your work on the theme. You have been given new eyes, new ears, even if only for a few moments, by your own and the group's work together. It can be helpful simply to let your mind rove over the various aspects of your life and find one to bless or understand with the added power that has come to you through meditation.

REPORTS OF THE MEDITATION

Reports of meditation are potentially the most beautiful aspect of group meditation. In the Quaker tradition, such reporting is supposed to follow the prompting of the Holy Spirit. It is an individualized form of the communal spirit of the gathering that informs one of the participants and makes him or her rise up and address the meeting.

Of course, we have problems with such reporting. For example, if you feel any pressure to report or any performance anxiety, then worries about what and whether to report may interrupt your closed-eyes meditation, quite self-defeatingly. There are other occupational hazards with which the following guidelines may help.

NO NEED TO REPORT

No one has to report. Nor do we need to take turns reporting in any sense. It is just that if you have something to say about what you experienced within the theme, you might decide to say it to the group when reports are called for.

Sometimes the greatest gift to the group is a simple, brief report, or the report that the theme came no closer. It is almost never a good idea to make a lengthy report. The greatest gift to the group might be to refrain from reporting. Often in a group there are those for whom it is a bit too easy to take the floor, and those for whom it is a bit too hard. Each would do well, occasionally at least, to play against type.

No Cross-talk

The report is a statement of what you experienced of the theme during the meditation. It is not the time to comment on the reports of others, or to have a new discussion of the theme, or to recall previous meditations and quotations. Each person who wants to speak does speak, and then a bit of silence lets what they have said sink in. Only after this respectful pause does the next person who wants to speak make a contribution about personal experience of the theme during meditation, without referring to the preceding reports.

Only Your Experience

When the meditation has been shallow or frustrating, it is best only to report that fact alone, or to keep silent. Instead, we are tempted to substitute borrowed profundities. But even the most beautiful memory or quotation is not what is needed just now. What is needed is your own experience, if you want to share it: your experience of the theme. Painful struggles with distractions, or perhaps amazing experiences of light and warmth, are equally beside the point. Let them go unreported. It's about your experience of the theme.

Sometimes it is hard to distinguish between a current experience of the theme and some past moment of revelation, or a beautiful story you recalled during the meditation. With good will and practice, the distinction becomes quite clear. One has the aroma of freshness about it, one has the smell of decay.

WHAT ABOUT LIVE EXPERIENCE?

It is conceivable that you feel the presence of the theme, with fresh understandings within it, just as you begin to report. If you speak to this current experience, it is akin to prophecy. It is no longer in the past tense even by so much as the distance between closed-eye meditation and the current moment of reporting. It is simultaneous meditation and speaking out, rather than about, this meditation. It is the Quaker ideal. By all means speak such current understanding, if it comes. Speak "as the spirit gives utterance."

But have a care. I have seen people in what they feel is this state who later acknowledge they got "carried away" and they were really rehashing beautiful ideas from elsewhere and before under the guise of prophecy. They were really just teaching. It was a lot of speculation, memory, aspiration, sentimentality—not current experience.

DO NOT PERSUADE

It is natural, though unhelpful, for us to try to convey the mood or intensity of our meditation when we report on it. We try to be emphatic or convincing, to get our actual experience across. There is no need. A simple account of what you have experienced of the theme is the only helpful contribution. Let your listeners supply the intensity; leave them free to accept or ignore your report.

So What's the Point of Reporting?

If there are so many caveats about reporting, why bother with it at all? If we are so likely to indulge, quote, discuss, speculate, and persuade, rather than truly report, is this phase, after all, best left out?

The reason to report actually has almost nothing to do with the reports or the reporter. The real work in the realm of reporting, and what makes it supremely valuable and worthwhile in spite of all the caveats, has to do with everyone else, the group listening to the report. For when we relate honestly our own most intimate experience of the theme, however humble it might be, we enable the listeners to find the theme in a new way just then, as they listen.

This is not because the report contains new information or some deep perspective. The benefits involved come about in an entirely different way. The report acts as a portal for the listeners to approach the theme afresh, and find out things about it that are neither in the reporter's experience nor in their own previous meditation. By filling the airwaves with speech and thought that is honest, relevant, and directly experienced, it is as if the reporter performs a special function for everyone else listening. The reporter invokes the theme by his or her true account, but also takes on the burden of linguistic production, so that the listeners are liberated to do something else with the part of their minds not involved in listening. This something else is a renewed feeling for the theme, which can grow in salience, liveliness, and revelatory power.

The phase of reporting, then, is a highly structured way for the listeners to continue their meditation. They can intensify it far beyond what was possible before. Listeners are focused, not so much on the content of the report and certainly not on any judgment of it. They are listening through the report for news of the theme.

CREATIVE REPORTS

Instead of simply recounting one's experience in natural language, reports can be sharpened by intentionally condensing them or undertaking alternative forms of responding to the meditation. This should be agreed upon in advance so that people are not disoriented at the time of reporting.

For example, participants can all take a moment, after the meditation and before anyone reports, to formulate a single sentence that encapsulates their experience. This will cut down on most of the overly verbose reports. They can make a haiku of their experience, or limit themselves to a six-word account. Again, they might report in the form of a quick drawing or painting if the materials are ready in advance.

Instead of any kind of report of the meditation, participants might say what the experience of the meditation will motivate them to undertake in their lives. For a decent meditation always carries with it a hint toward the future, a task of some kind, even if only the feeling, "It's high time to deepen my meditative practice." This is the style of Rilke, in his "Archaic Torso of Apollo," wherein he describes the sculpture in some detail, marveling at its secrets, and then suddenly breaks off with the comment, "You must change your life."

Our reception of these creative responses is also best when non-evaluative. Listening to them, seeing them, feeling them, our aim is still, as ever, to become more intimate with the meditative theme: nothing else.

Restatement of the Theme

Stella Elliston, a member of a western Massachusetts group, invented the technique of restating the meditation theme after the last report. This means that someone, maybe someone who did not state the theme at the beginning or someone who did not report, simply says the theme out loud to close the session. If the theme is an image, a story, or a physical object, it can be very briefly re-presented to the group.

When we hear the theme repeated after our group work, it resonates with all that we have done. It has an almost palpable weight or import that certainly was not there when the whole procedure began. We may notice that, to the degree the group as a whole gave itself to the theme, the theme has become something personally powerful. It implicates us. It has become a part of us, and we of it. The atmosphere of the room has changed. We are all the more incarnate, but now more palpably accompanied. The sensation can come that this is a feast, and we have now, at last, been adequately fed.

Theme and Variations

One flexible form of group meditative practice has been given above. It remains open. Every aspect of this form is up for grabs, that is, for creative innovation, so that it can be a generative center from which many, even unrecognizably different, forms can arise.

For example, the group might agree to meet one week in simple silence, with no specific instruction or theme. This is the ultimate theme, in a sense, leaving everyone on their own completely, as in a Quaker meeting.

Unless they are very practiced, however, most participants will enter this kind of session incapable of inner silence. They need something to "chew" on, and so tend to bounce from theme to theme inwardly—perhaps not a bad way to fill the time, but very prone to distraction.

Sometimes, as soon as the theme is announced, its presence or power is felt in the room. A practiced group might then launch into closed-eye meditation on the theme without prior discussion. The place of discussion has been filled by the felt fact of the theme's approach.

This means getting a feeling for the meditation theme and forgetting about its words or images almost immediately. We then concentrate on the theme-specific feeling itself: the feeling is the theme. It also means a refusal to "think" about the theme in any ordinary sense from the very first, while remaining with its inner momentum.

Groups all too easily put authority for the theme in the hands of one or just a few group members. This tends to encourage the "non-leaders" in a certain passivity. It can be helpful for the group members each to take turns preparing the theme in advance for the session and then presenting the theme to the group. This could be either an introduction to the group discussion or a replacement for discussion.

We can alternate kinds of meditation to refresh our capacity for focus and to get the gesture of logos-oriented practice more clearly. So we pick a theme one week; the next week we simply focus on the breath; then we return to a theme on the following week, and so on. Some of the same benefit can come by simply preceding the theme-based meditation each time with a period of breath focus or with walking meditation, as in the Vipassana tradition. In this mindful walking, which should be very slow, you focus on the physical sensations in the moving foot and leg while walking slowly and consciously. It can be undertaken as "three-part walking," with a focus first on the will movement of the lifting heel, then the feeling-quality of the foot in floating motion, then the decisive thinking quality of foot-placement. As with all meditative practice, we lightly turn from distractions back to the task at hand. One sneaky distraction is the temptation to rush, as if it were about getting to the end of the room. But this exercise has nothing to do with efficiency of locomotion. When we then turn from the breath or from walking to the day's theme, we feel intensely the specific mission of theme-based meditation.

It may set the tone to read aloud a verse or prayer at the start of the procedure, or even as a willed interruption, to bring people's scattered energies to the room. Read it twice, as an invitation truly to slow down, gather yourselves, and begin to swim within the currents of meaning.

In our time, we suffer from a rock-solid identification with the eyes and the brain, as if they were the seat of the person. Small children, people in archaic cultures, and we ourselves in many altered states, all demonstrate that this is not a necessary condition. The center of the person is shiftable, and not always spatial. We can try a simple imaginal exercise to refresh our sense of self and world by bringing our thinking of the theme, spatially, as if from the head down physically into the heart. We allow ourselves to experience the images or words of the theme as if they originate in the center of the chest. This helps us to come unstuck from our habitual ways of thinking and feeling.

At times, we can declare that there will be no reporting that day. We may then notice as we meditate how, at other times, we were always partly planning what we were going to report and so wasting some of the energy that could have gone into the theme. This practice helps us, on subsequent occasions, when there will be reporting again, to renounce any cares about reporting. A helpful slogan for meditants, with regard to reporting and much else: "If I'm here now, I'll be there then."

We can also agree to begin or end the session in silence, all together, even filing out in the end without saying good-bye. Any such reduction in meaningless speech helps, at the beginning of our time together, to gather the power of the theme. At the end of our meeting, it tends to preserve the benefits of the meditation.

We can make reports on the current session's meditation not now, but at the beginning of the next session.

We can report by offering a newly invented prayer, poem, or dance.

Obviously, we don't want to be the slaves of form. The consistency of meditative practice comes not from any fixed form, but from other essential elements. These include return from distraction as concentration deepens, the repeated orientation toward intensity of being, intentional intimacy or non-duality with the theme, and the logos-principle of meaning.

All the above variations to the form of group meditation, and an infinity of others, are available for experiment. On the one hand, any style or form needs to be held to for a time to learn its ins and outs, its virtues and hazards. This consideration would have us stick loyally to one form. On the other hand, forms tend to become stifling, and we all too easily mistake the bottle for the wine. This consideration argues for change.

SENSE OF THE GROUP

In Quaker practice, a meeting is known as "gathered" when an overlighting presence is felt, a presence that unites the participants with the inside of the world—"a sense sublime / Of something far more deeply interfused." Thomas Kelly, in his classic Quaker pamphlet, "The Gathered Meeting," points up some of the special characteristics of these relatively rare and always astonishing group phenomena.

One of the most central is that, as the group feels close to the sources of being it also feels unified and intimate within itself. Kelly says, "It occurs again and again that two or three individuals find the boundaries of their separateness partially melted down." He mentions "two or three individuals" here, quoting of course from Matthew 18:20, "For where two or three are gathered together in my name, there am I in the midst of them."

Readers of this book will be able to supply the truly mysterious and also frankly practical interpretation of this famous sentence. "My name" does not mean, for instance, anything like "Jesus Christ" as the name of a human or God, but rather the I AM itself, being itself, the very possibility that there could be anything or anyone—YHWH. So Jesus is saying that when concentration on a theme has become intense enough, when we are gathered in the name, or the urge of incarnation itself, then that ground of being that brings each of us into existence, the very ground of being that brings all else into existence as well, comes to the forefront of evidence. (By the way, *Jesus* means, etymologically, "Being saves.")

It is significant that Kelly, who describes the experience of a gathered meeting with such exact familiarity, is impressed by the fact, as he puts it, that "the experience has a knowledge quality." He notes that even though we do not emerge from a group meditation with "a single crisp sentence or judgment of capsuled knowledge," yet now, "the secrets of this amazing world have been in some larger degree laid bare." We feel that we are seeing not just the outer image of reality's tapestry, but the other side, the weave-side, as well. We discover the weaver at work, or even that we ourselves are this weaver of reality's warp and weft.

All of this accounts for the tremendous help that others' presence gives us in meditation. For people routinely say that it goes better with others than when they try to meditate alone. The aid others give us by their presence in meditation goes beyond the help given by the presence of others on a sports team, for instance, or collaborating on a project. There, the good faith and good will of others keep us on task and spur us to do more, even through competition. In a meditative group, something further is at play.

Kelly says, "The Real Presence of the gathered meeting is all existential fact." That is, rather than something as airy as knowledge in the normal sense, the group's presence to one another strikes each participant as a fact, a deed, a world event as undeniable as any we can conceive. Simply put, the meditants become more real to each other. This increase can lead to an upward spiral in the felt sense of reality altogether.

Often, in daily life, we cannot meet one another's gaze. "Good eye contact" has become a byword in business relations. Its absence is often mentioned as a symptom of psychopathology. But why exactly is it hard to meet the gaze of another human being?

To answer this question, we can take a detour and ask another. Why do people deny the fact of parting? For example, if someone leaves a business to go to another job, his or her colleagues routinely pretend that the separation is not really taking place. People say a cheerful, "See you around!," when they know perfectly well that this won't happen. They say, "Don't be a stranger, give a shout, shoot me an e-mail," and so on. Why are we unable simply to say, "This is it. Good-bye. I wish you well"? What is going on here?

What we cannot face in any parting is not actually the threat of absence, but the threat of presence. We find it almost unbearable to face the "hello" that would be there in a real "good-bye." It would be an act of meeting, a meeting perhaps more intense than any that happened in our years of work together. The other person, the moment, our presence to one another, would be felt in that encounter, and it is too great to bear.

Now we can return to the original question about eye contact. For in every slight eye-contact the possibility of encountering the whole of the other person is there. In such a real meeting, we ourselves will be asked to be present, and will in fact become present. So it is a challenge both on the receptive and expressive sides: to perceive more of the other, and to be more available oneself.

In what sense is this meeting "too much"? William Blake said, "We are put on Earth a little space, that we may learn to bear the beams of love." But why, if love is good, don't we just lap it up? Why is it hard to bear these beams? We are back to the problem of "too good to be true."

The lines of our attention are normally turned backward, toward our separate selves. It is this chronic gesture of pointing selfward that makes us identify with, and anxious about, our boundaries. Paradoxically, every self-protective gesture of this kind makes us weaker in the presence of another being. Only love trained outward can endure the beauty of a true encounter. Rilke said the angels are terrifying, but any human being will do very well for our difficulty with glory. As the lines of outwardly, upwardly directed attention grow strong with intentional focus, as we develop our powers of concentration and true feeling, encounter from face to face becomes more and more possible. We awaken at the boundaries, neither cowering within them nor abandoning them. We awaken to the fact of being, which is our ultimate source of connection and strength, and the fountain of all generosity. We find that to endure the other as other is also the likeliest way to know the other as oneself. The vastness of the other person, the radiance of the theme, and the miracle of being, all become good news we can endure—and even declare.

Sample Themes

There are an infinite number of possible meditative themes. Here are a few favorites:

Sentences

- Who gives, receives. (Georg Kühlewind)
- I am a child of Earth and the starry heavens, but my home is in the heavens. (Orphic tablet at Petelia)
- The desire for light produces it. (Simone Weil)
- Every moment is a little door through which the messiah could enter. (Walter Benjamin)
- Except a corn of wheat fall into the Earth and die, it abideth alone. But if it die, it bringeth forth much fruit. (John: 12:23)
- This mind is the Buddha. (Mahayana aphorism)
- From the first, not a thing is. (Mahayana aphorism)
- I experience myself, thinking, at one with the stream of the world-process. (Rudol Steiner)
- Man is a stream whose source is hidden. (Ralph Waldo Emerson)
- What was your original face before your parents were born? (Zen koan)
- Happy is the man who walks in the way of being. (Psalm 1)
- My cup runneth over. (Psalm 23)
- Behold, I make all new. (Rev: 21:5)
- One day you will know: a god felt you now. (Rudolf Steiner)
- The Tree of Eternity has its roots in Heaven and its branches reach down to the Earth. (Katha Upanishad)
- We are always in the light. (Georg Kühlewind)

- With man this is not possible, but with God all things are possible. (Matthew 19:26)
- Buddha means aware, miraculously aware (Bodhidharma)
- Are you ready? (Massimo Scaligero)

Images

- The crucifixion
- The Rose Cross (cf. Rudolf Steiner, *An Outline of Esoteric Science*, pp. 340–341)
- The Star of David (triangle pointing up and triangle pointing down)
- A tree planted by a stream (Psalm 1)
- The Buddha seated under the Bodhi Tree
- Buddha handing the flower to Kasyapa (Flower Sermon)

Stories/Events

- Healing stories from the Gospels (e.g., John 5:1–9)
- Jataka Tales (e.g. in Noor Inayat Khan's *Twenty Jataka Tales*)
- Zen stories (e.g. in Katsuki Sekida, trans., *Blue Cliff Record,* cases 1 and 55; or in Paul Reps, *Zen Flesh, Zen Bones*)
- Tales of the Desert Fathers (e.g., in Waddell and Pennington, *The Desert Fathers*)
- Hasidic Tales (e.g., in *The Hasidic Anthology,* Louis I. Newman)
- Bhagavad Gita

BIBLIOGRAPHY

Kühlewind, Georg, *From Normal to Healthy: Paths to the Liberation of Consciousness,* Great Barrington, MA: Lindisfarne Books, 1988.

———. *The Light of the "I": Guidelines for Meditation,* Great Barrington, MA: Lindisfarne Books, 2008.

Inayat Khan, Noor, *Twenty Jataka Tales,* Rochester, VT: Inner Traditions, 1985.

Kelly, Thomas R., "The Gathered Meeting," in *The Eternal Promise: A Sequal to "A Testament of Devotion,"* New York: Harper & Row, 1966.

Lipson, Michael, *Stairway of Surprise: Six Steps to a Creative Life,* Great Barrington, MA: Lindisfarne Books, 2002.

Newman, Louis I., The *Hasidic Anthology: Tales of the Hasidim,* New York: Schocken Books, 1963.

Novalis, *Hymns to the Night / Spiritual Songs,* London: Temple Lodge, 2001.

Reps, Paul, and Nyogen Senzaki, *Zen Flesh, Zen Bones: A Collection of Zen and Pre-Zen Writings,* Boston: Tuttle, 1985.

Scaligero, Massimo, *The Light (La Luce): An Introduction to Creative Imagination,* Great Barrington, MA: Lindisfarne Books, 2001.

Sekida, Katsuki, trans., *Two Zen Classics: The Gateless Gate and the Blue Cliff Records,* Boston: Shambhala, 2005.

Steiner, Rudolf, *How to Know Higher Worlds: A Modern Path of Initiation,* Hudson, NY: Anthroposophic Press, 1994.

———. *An Outline of Esoteric Science,* Hudson, NY: Anthroposophic Press, 1997.

Waddell, Helen, and Basil Pennington, *The Desert Fathers,* New York: Vintage Classics, 1998.

THANKS

Thanks to all who contributed to this book. The generous helpers toward this project are too many to name or enumerate, but I cannot resist a few.

First, thanks to my father, Leon Lipson, who introduced me to the concept of meditation when I was seven. And to my mother, Dorothy Ann, who made me care.

Thanks to my grandmother, Fanny Rapoport, who showed me lightheartedness through all the upping and downing of life.

Thanks to my brother and sister, James and Abigail, without whose fierce, challenging intelligence I would have developed into mush.

Thanks to Georg Kühlewind, who brought me back from apathy to interest when I was twenty-two, and who showed so many of us how to enter the open heavens.

Fred Paddock and Claire Hicks, M.D., have both dared me to look at Being from ever-new angles. This offering owes immeasurably to the instruction of their friendship. Thanks to David Spangler, whose teaching gives Earth its full, amazing radiance, and who makes the word *friend* into a full meal.

Thanks to Chris Bamford, friend and fire-bringer, and everyone at SteinerBooks, above all Gene Gollogly, Mary Giddens, Jens Jensen, Marsha Post and Stephan O'Reilly. You incarnate the word both professionally and selflessly!

Thanks to Ross Bleckner, who so graciously allowed me to use his painting, *Galaxy with Birds,* for the cover.

Thanks to my children, Asher and Rody, who convince me there will be a smiling future.

Thanks (more than to any one) to Holly Morse, my life-long teacher and model of love in action. She makes the universe possible.

And thanks to the hundreds who, over the years, have meditated with me in groups. You have shown me, again and again, the unfathomable beauty of the human heart.